D0948195

Tennessee County History Series

TENNESSEE COUNTY HISTORY SERIES

Morgan County

by W. Calvin Dickinson

Frank B. Williams, Jr.

Editor

MEMPHIS STATE UNIVERSITY PRESS

Memphis, Tennessee

Maps prepared by Reaves & Sweeney, Inc.

Manufactured in the United States of America

Designed by Gary G. Gore

ISBN 0-87870-157-5

Preface

While working on this book, I was frequently asked, "Where is Morgan County?" The easiest answer was, "Brushy Mountain Prison is in Morgan County." That answer generated a sign of recognition on the face of the inquirer. Other landmarks in the county are not so readily recognized. Rugby, which achieved some national and international notoriety, is not usually associated with Morgan County. Even Sam Smith, in his *Tennessee History: A Bibliography,* put Rugby in Fentress County.

One of the purposes of this county history series is to acquaint Tennessee citizens and other Americans with the local history of our state. All of our counties have a rich and colorful history, and one can only appreciate any area when he knows and understands the history of that place.

One can drive through Morgan County and immediately appreciate the natural beauty of the area, unsurpassed anywhere. It was this natural beauty that lured many of the inhabitants to the county. But one must look deeper, at the history of the county, to understand its human beauty. Economic wealth is not prevalent; one does not gasp at material memorials to human achievement. One must examine the written word—history—to realize the accomplishments of the people. Morgan County's natural beauty masks difficult natural problems; the hardships the people faced, the hard work they endured, and the heartbreak they suffered create the heartwarming story of the county's history.

In researching and writing Morgan County's history I came to know, to appreciate, and to identify with the problems and the progress of the people. The inhabitants of the county don't know me, but I know them. I know their names, their families, their homes, their work, and their play. I know their history, and I appreciate and honor them. I identify with Morgan County. In the same way, I hope that anyone who reads this history will recognize and appreciate the abilities and the achievements of the men and women who made the history of Morgan County.

To thank people is easy, and maybe many times too lightly done. My debt to individuals who helped me complete this book is large, and I am most aware that the book's value would be considerably less without their advice and assistance. As author I must assume responsibility for any shortcomings. The individuals below did not contribute any of those; they eliminated some which you don't find, and they made the book more readable and more factually correct than it otherwise would have been.

My heaviest debt is to Mrs. Glena Kreis Ott, deceased, and Miss Ethel Freytag. The research that they did in preparation for their *A History of Morgan County Tennessee* was invaluable in my work on this book. They did so much of the "courthouse" work which is so time consuming, yet so necessary. The county can never thank them enough for searching out and preserving its history.

Mr. Charles Kreis also deserves the gratitude of the county, in addition to my gratitude, for saving the county's history. His extensive collection of photographs, so lovingly collected and preserved, was the source of most of the illustrations in this book. His reading of the manuscript made the book more valuable as a historical document. His love for the county and its history is obvious in the care that he took to improve this manuscript.

Judy Cooper, editor of the *Morgan County News,* was very generous with her time and her resources, spending hours helping me find people and material. Steve Jacks, staff member at Brushy Mountain Prison, also was generous with his time and knowledge, acquainting me with the prison and its part in the county's history.

Dr. Larry Whiteaker of the Tennessee Tech History Department played a valuable double role in the publication of this book. As noted in the text, he wrote the account of Morgan County's part in the Civil War. He is a recognized authority in this subject, and I appreciate his willingness to contribute his expertise to the manuscript. Then he went the extra mile and volunteered to edit the manuscript for improvement of style. It was my good fortune to have a second editor, Ms. Gail Adcock. She and Dr. Whiteaker gave the book its quality of style.

Tennessee County History Series

MORGAN County is part of the Cumberland Plateau region of East Tennessee. The plateau lies diagonally across the state from north to south and comprises the westernmost section of East Tennessee, dividing East Tennessee from Middle Tennessee.

Modern Morgan County consists of 344,960 acres, or 539 square miles. It has a rectangular shape, 30 miles long and 20 miles wide. It was created in 1817 out of Roane and Anderson counties. Fentress County (1823), Scott County (1849), and Cumberland County (1855) were later formed partly out of Morgan County, and their creation gave Morgan County its modern size, shape, and neighbors.

The geography of Morgan County explains its history. It is rugged country, its surface divided into two sections. Seventy-five percent of the county is part of the Cumberland Plateau, and the southeast quarter is the eastern extent of the Cumberland Mountains. The plateau is a rolling tableland with an average elevation of 100 feet above adjacent lands and 1700 to 2000 feet above sea level. The mountains rise about 1000 feet above the plateau. These mountains consist of narrow ridges with steep sides deeply scarred by water. Fodderstack and Frozen Head are the highest points in the county at more than 3000

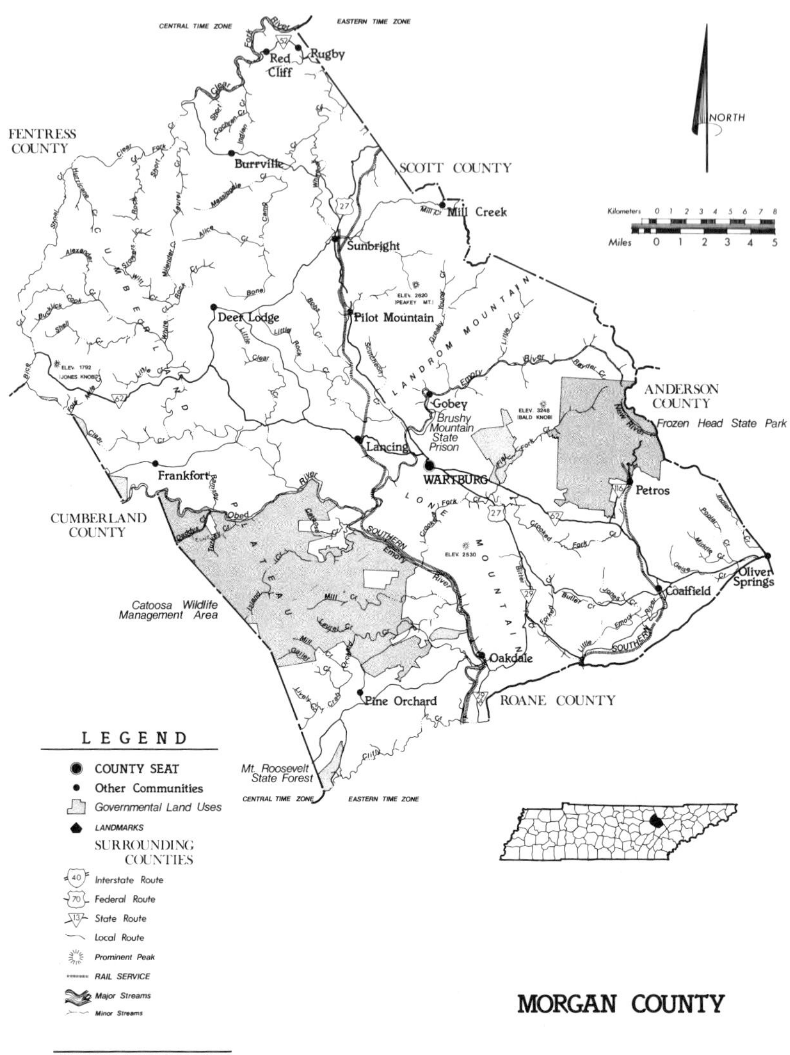
MORGAN COUNTY
CENTRAL TIME ZONE
EASTERN TIME ZONE
NORTH
Kilometers 0 1 2 3 4 5 6 7 8
Miles 0 1 2 3 4 5
FENTRESS COUNTY
SCOTT COUNTY
ANDERSON COUNTY
CUMBERLAND COUNTY
ROANE COUNTY
Red Cliff
Rugby
Burrville
Mill Creek
Sunbright
Pilot Mountain
Deer Lodge
Gobey
Brushy Mountain State Prison
Lancing
WARTBURG
Frankfort
Petros
Coalfield
Oliver Springs
Oakdale
Pine Orchard
Frozen Head State Park
Catoosa Wildlife Management Area
Mt. Roosevelt State Forest
ELEV. 2620 (PEAKEY MT.)
ELEV. 1792 (JONES KNOB)
ELEV. 3248 (BALD KNOB)
ELEV. 2530
LANDROM MOUNTAIN
LONE MOUNTAIN
CUMBERLAND PLATEAU
SOUTHERN
LEGEND
COUNTY SEAT
Other Communities
Governmental Land Uses
LANDMARKS
SURROUNDING COUNTIES
Interstate Route
Federal Route
State Route
Local Route
Prominent Peak
RAIL SERVICE
Major Streams
Minor Streams
SOURCE: Tennessee Department of Transportation

feet. Gaps in Walden Ridge (named for Elisha Walden, who explored this area as early as 1761) at Harriman, De Armond, and Oliver Springs provide the only access to the county from the southeast. Railroads were built through each of these gaps. New River Gap at Petros provides another route from the east. The high, rugged, and difficult terrain on the east, the direction from which most early settler and trade traffic would come, made the development of the county slow and difficult.

Two rivers in the county are Emory and Obed. The Obed, with its tributaries Clear Creek and Daddy's Creek, drains into the Emory from Cumberland County to the west. The Emory (spelled "Emery" in earlier texts) flows from the eastern part of the county, draining south into the Clinch River in Roane County. Crooked Fork and Flat Fork are tributaries of the Emory. These rivers and various creeks cut deeply into the surface, sometimes as much as 500 feet. Although the easiest form of travel in the early part of the nineteenth century was by water, Morgan County was denied this luxury. Even though the Emory empties into the Clinch and the Clinch into the Tennessee, the Emory itself does not carry enough water to allow shipping except near its mouth. The creeks in the northern part of the county—Clear Fork, White Oak, Black Wolf, and Brimstone—spill into the Big South Fork of the Cumberland; but none of these creeks has the water volume to support shipping. The rough terrain and inadequate water made travel so difficult in Morgan County that settlement and development were extremely slow. The barrier effect of bordering escarpments discouraged entrance into the area. Internal land travel was hampered by mountains in the southeast and by stream gorges on the plateau.

Of the nearly 345,000 acres in the county, only 900 acres have soil that is "well suited" for farming; 29,500 acres are "suited" for farming. Almost half of the county—182,000 acres—is "unsuited" for cultivation. The soil is acidic, low in organic matter, and deficient in plant nutrients. Heavy application of fertilizer is necessary to produce most agricultural crops. The steeply sloping land in much of the county provides another impediment to successful agriculture. In the nineteenth century farmers planted crops that were unsuited to the soil and climate of the county; the crop failures combined with absence of markets and poor travel conditions further explain the slow economic development of the county. Livestock finally became the most profitable agrarian enterprise.

The most abundant natural resources in Morgan County are timber and coal. Forests blanket 89 percent of the county. The mountains in the eastern part are covered with hardwood, and the plateau grows a mixture of pine and hardwood. The harvest and use of this timber would eventually provide a large amount of the county's revenue. Coal, though, would be the "black gold" of the county, providing revenue and jobs through the middle of the twentieth century. The Cumberland Plateau contains the only coal in the state of Tennessee, producing two percent of the country's supply. Much of it is bituminous rank coal of coking quality from the Pennsylvanian Age rock underlying the plateau. In Morgan County most of the mineable coal is in the Crooked Fork, Slatestone, Indian Bluff, Graves Gap, and Redrock Mountain groups, with three quarters of the recoverable seams in the Crooked Fork and Redrock Mountain groups.

The natural beauty of the mountains and the plateau regions of Morgan County are its hope for economic prosperity in the future. It was basically this wealth of nature that was used by advertisements in the nineteenth century to lure settlers from Europe and the United States into the area. It was primarily the natural beauty of the place that travelers and early settlers praised. Health resorts thrived in the later nineteenth century, drawing upon the scenic beauty of the area as a health advertisement. Many of the early settlers were sadly deceived by this facade of beauty, for underneath its lure, Morgan County proved to be a difficult place to live. This would continue to be the case even after railroads and highways solved the severe travel problems and after science moderated the agrarian problems.

Indians and Settlers

There is no evidence that modern Indians maintained permanent settlements in Morgan County, although it was a part of their hunting territory. In 1799 some Moravian missionaries traveling from Knoxville to Nashville through Southwest Point (Kingston) and Crab Orchard referred to the area west of the Clinch River as "wilderness." It was "a stretch of country entirely uninhabited."

Four Indian burial mounds on the Emory River above Gobey were probably related to Indians of the period before European exploration and settlement of North America. They were called Woodland Indians, and they flourished between 1000 B.C. and 1000 A.D. The Cherokees were ignorant of the origin of the mounds.

In the eighteenth century Indians lived south of Morgan County, and they used the county's lands as hunting grounds. There may have been a few Indians living in Morgan County in the nineteenth century. Indian Tavern was supposedly named because some Cherokees lived in the vicinity. William R. Nelson, an herb doctor who lived in Morgan County, said that some Cherokees lived in cabins on the Cumberland Plateau, and from them he learned his tricks of healing.

In 1805 the Third Treaty of Tellico took Morgan County and the surrounding territory away from the Cherokees in exchange for $14,000 and a $3000 annuity. The negotiating chiefs were bribed in secret articles of the treaty by offers of large tracts of land.

The first permanent white settlers moved into Morgan County immediately after the Tellico Treaty. The Hall brothers, Samuel and Martin, may have been the first in 1807–1808. Samuel settled northeast of where Wartburg would later be located, and Martin moved into the same vicinity on Lower Flat Fork Creek. The Stonecipherss—David, Joseph, Benjamin, and Ezra—closely followed the Halls. The first three settled on Crooked Fork Creek, and Ezra located on Beech Fork. Elijah Reese and Titus England took land on Flat Fork Creek in 1808.

The Samuel Hall house on the Emory River northeast of Wartburg. Built about 1808, the log house covered with clapboard was the first house in Morgan County. (Courtesy of Charles Kreis)

John Freels located on White Oak Creek in 1811, and Royal Price on Clear Creek in 1812. John Staples brought his large family to the south side of the Emory in 1814. Other pioneer settlers who came to the area before Morgan County was created in 1817 were John Brasel, Littleburg Brient, Jesse Casey, John Craig, William Davidson, Ephraim Davis, Zachariah Embree, Jeremiah Hatfield, Hartsell Hurt, Squire and Morgan Hendricks, Basil Human, Jacob and John Laymance, Robert McCartt, Charles and Andrew Prewitt, Lewis Rector, Andrew Shannon, Nicholas Summers, John Webb, Charles Williams, and Mathias Williams. Most of them settled along the county's creeks and rivers to be near water supplies and food.

A number of settlers who moved to Morgan County were Revolutionary War veterans who received land grants from North Carolina when Tennessee was still the western extension of that state. W. L. E. Davidson, Housely Human, Charles

McClung, Isaiah Patton, Tobias Peters, and the Alley and Sexton families claimed land with such grants. In the first half of the nineteenth century at least thirty-two veterans lived in Morgan County. Seventeen of these settlers had come from North Carolina, eight from Virginia, and three from South Carolina.

These early settlers lived in rural isolation, practicing an economy based on abundant game, subsistence farming, and husbandry. A. B. Wright, who was born on the Wolf River in neighboring Fentress County two decades after Morgan County's first settlers arrived, described the primitive mode of life in the area. His family lived in a log cabin because the material was free, because log cabins were easily constructed by a person with few carpentry skills, and because sawmills had not been brought into the area to provide milled lumber. Cooking stoves were unavailable in the area, so meals were prepared at the open fire or fireplace. Deer and bear were plentiful, and turkeys roamed in large flocks; so game provided a ready supplement to farm animals, or might provide the only protein for a poor family. Small grain was grown on plots; it was gathered with a reaping hook and thrashed by horses walking on it.

Two roads, primitive by modern standards, passed through the area before these first settlers arrived. They made passage into and through this difficult region easier, provided ingress for the settlers, and made their lives somewhat less isolated. The Nashville-Knoxville Turnpike provided the first route. It passed through the gap at Oliver Springs and ran northwest through Morgan County into what is now Fentress County. The first county seat of Morgan County, old Montgomery, was on this road, and the roadbed is still visible near the site of the town west of Lancing. The second Montgomery was also on this turnpike, east of the first site.

Walton Road, begun in 1799 and completed in 1802, did not pass through modern Morgan County. Although deeds filed in Morgan County in the 1830s used the Walton Road as a reference, these lands lay in the southwestern part, which became Cumberland County in 1855. Early travelers' accounts, as well as faint traces of the road still extant near Daysville and Ozone, definitely indicate that the road passed just south of the modern boundary of Morgan County. Nevertheless, travelers could, and must have, used Walton's Road to travel toward Morgan County. A comparatively easy road, except for difficult points like Spencer's Mountain, it accommodated the wagon traffic necessary for settlers moving their possessions. It was 15 feet wide across flat land and 12 feet wide through the mountains. The surface was leveled by shovel, and bridges were built across the streams and rivers. There were a number of inns or "stands" along the road.

Supplementing these early east-west roads in Morgan County were numerous turnpikes built during the nineteenth century. Stock companies built these roads as profit-making enterprises. Tolls were collected to reimburse and recompense the stockholders. The tolls charged on one turnpike in Morgan County ranged from 60¢ for a wagon and six horses to 1¢ for a sheep or hog. This turnpike charged no toll for humans, but only for wagons and carriages or animals. Walton Road tollgate keepers charged for persons in addition to wagons and animals. Neither collected for persons walking. After 1879 tollgate keepers could not collect from persons going to elections, to church, or to mills.

Piles (or Pyles) Turnpike was the first constructed in Morgan County, in 1805 or 1806. This is a logical date for the first local road, since settlers were just coming into the area. This road began at the head of Poplar Creek and moved through Morgan County to the Wolf River. It became an important beginning or termination point for other roads in the county. Marchbanks Turnpike, built in 1835, was an important east-west toll road. It passed through Morgan County by way of the second Montgomery, through the later Cumberland County near Bledsoe Stand and Officer Stand, and westward to Carthage. Davidson's Turnpikes (1815 & 1817), Butler's Turnpike (1817), Officer's Turnpike (1819), Marney's Turnpike (1832), Taylor-Simpson Turnpike (1836), Tandy Center Turnpike (1841), David Smith Turnpike (1842), Scott's Turnpike (1844), Montgomery Turnpike (1848), and Big Emory Turnpike (1850) were all commissioned in Morgan County by the middle of the century. Others were built after 1850.

County Creation

In 1817 the Tennessee legislature created Morgan as the 39th county of the state, its territory sliced mostly out of Roane County to the south. Morgan County began on Walden's Ridge on the line of Roane and Anderson counties, then ran southwest along the top of the ridge. From where the Great Cumberland Road crossed the ridge, the county line ran to the Clear Fork of the Cumberland River, then due north to the Kentucky line. On the Kentucky line Morgan County joined the Campbell County line to the east. About 1600 inhabitants lived in the area at the time of the county's creation.

The new county was named in memory of Brigadier General Daniel Morgan, who died in 1802. (The legislative act that created Morgan County mistakenly ranked Morgan as a Major General). Morgan was born in New Jersey in 1736 and moved to Virginia at age 17. He was a wagoner attached to Braddock's army in that disastrous expedition to western Pennsylvania during the French and Indian War. In the Revolutionary War he served under Benedict Arnold in the assault on Quebec in 1775; he was with General Horatio Gates at the battle of Saratoga in 1777; and he defeated the British at Cowpens in South Carolina in 1781. Some soldiers from eastern Tennessee probably served with Morgan at Cowpens, and some veterans of his army might have received land grants in the county named after him.

The enactment that created Morgan County named five commissioners—William Davidson, Daniel S. Lavender, Lewis Rector, Elijah Rice, and John Triplet—who were to choose a site for the county seat. It was to be situated at "the most convenient" location in the county, at which place they were to purchase about 40 acres on which to build the town. Streets were to be laid off, with two acres near the center reserved for courthouse, prison, and stocks.

The legislature directed that the county seat be named Montgomery, in honor of Major Lemuel P. Montgomery, although one historian has claimed that the town was named for Hugh M. Montgomery, surveyor who laid out the town site. Lemuel Montgomery was born in Virginia in 1786, but his family moved to Knoxville, Tennessee, during his youth. He studied law in a judge's office in Knoxville and established a practice in Nashville. Appointed a major by President Madison, he was killed mounting the breastworks at the Battle of Horseshoe Bend during General Jackson's campaign against the Creek and Cherokee Indians in 1814.

The commissioners were to auction lots in Montgomery and use the proceeds to finance construction of a courthouse and a jail. If land sales did not supply sufficient funds to finance these buildings, the commissioners could tax county residents up to 12¼ cents per hundred acres.

Commissioner Daniel Lavender thwarted the legislature's instructions that the commissioners select and buy suitable land for the county seat. He donated land of undetermined acreage on the Nashville-Knoxville Turnpike about 13 miles west of modern Wartburg. The county built a small log courthouse and a log jail on the site in 1819. Nothing remains of this first Montgomery except a large pile of stones which may have been the courthouse chimney.

County administration was directed by the commissioners, now called justices of the peace, who held quarter sessions and courts of pleas.

The first session of Morgan County Court convened in January of 1818. The log courthouse was not complete at that time, so the court gathered in Indian Tavern, with William Davidson presiding. (Some authors have confused Davidson with General William Lee Davidson of North Carolina, who died in 1781 at the Battle of Cowan's Ford. Davidson County, Tennessee, is named for him.) Abraham M'Clellan and/or Solomon Geran attended to qualify the members of the court. In addition to this ceremony, the court recorded one transfer of land. Charles McClung conveyed 149 acres of land on the Little Emory River to Robert Williams for the sum of $298. William Wall, Morgan

County Clerk of Court, witnessed, signed, and sealed the deed, the first recorded in the new county.

Court records from the 1820s indicate a broad range of work that the justices undertook. They heard both criminal and civil cases, appointed deputy sheriffs and overseers of roads, granted licenses for taverns or inns, granted support for the poor, and paid bounties for killing wolves. The justices also assumed responsibility for orphans. Parentless children were "bound" to a person for care. The person named made bond, promised not to abuse the child, and to care for him until age 21. In return, the child worked for the person. The county court set the tax rate, which was 31 cents on each hundred acres of land in 1824. James McIntosh, whose job as sheriff in 1824 included collecting taxes, was found to be in default in that year for the sum of $217.78, plus $20.91 of poor tax money. McIntosh resigned his position, but there is no record of additional punishment.

In addition to the sheriff and his deputies, peace in the county was maintained by seven militia companies. Morgan County was home to the 30th Regiment of the state militia, and each of the seven companies in this regiment was commanded by a captain, two lieutenants, and one ensign. Three sergeants, three corporals, and at least 45 privates made up the ranks of a company. Members of each company reported twice a year for muster and drill. In 1825 the company captains in Morgan County were Baldwin, Barwick, Davidson, Doherty, Hughes, Myatt, and Spicer.

In 1823 Fentress County was created, partly out of the western section of Morgan County. So much of Morgan was taken that Montgomery was no longer near the geographical center of the county. In 1825 the Tenneseee Legislature granted permission for the county seat to be moved east to a more central location and directed that the name of the new town be Montgomery. The commissioners appointed to purchase the site and erect public buildings were Jacob Laymance (Chairman), John England, Benjamin Hagler, John Prescott, Samuel Scott, Shadrack Stephens, and Sterling Williams.

The commissioners selected ten acres on the east side of the

Emory River on the Nashville-Knoxville Turnpike, about one mile west of modern Wartburg. William Wall, County Court Clerk, sold the land to the county for $40. Some of the individual lots in the ten acres sold for $200 each about ten years later. Samuel Scott, one of the commissioners, owned most of the land surrounding the town.

John Staples, county surveyor, laid out the second, or new, Montgomery in 1826. It consisted of 13 half-acre lots and a one-acre public square. Robert Bush, a free Negro blacksmith, bought the first lot. Constantine Braus, John Brient, James Johnson, and William Staples all bought lots and opened businesses. Thomas S. Lea, a physician, opened an office, as did Levi Trewhitt, a lawyer. A tanyard and a tobacco factory were early industries in Montgomery.

The county government constructed a temporary courthouse and jail on the public square. In 1851 they built a new jail, and the next year the court appointed commissioners to supervise construction of a new courthouse. This structure was never completed.

In the 1830s Walden's Academy, chartered by the state in 1827, operated in Montgomery as a teacher training school. The county owned and operated the institution, which was housed in a two-story frame building at the rear of the courthouse. Hugh Montgomery, Thomas Scruggs, and G. W. Keith served as instructors. Walden's Academy continued until at least 1870, and in 1877 another school with the same name was incorporated.

The Methodists owned a meeting house in Montgomery which was on the circuit of A. B. Wright, Methodist preacher in the area around 1870.

One tavern on the turnpike that ran through Montgomery was Ye Olde Tavern, operated by Justice of the Peace Samuel Scott until his death in 1841. Then his son Julian controlled the inn, which boasted 19 beds to accommodate travelers. Scott owned several slaves who constituted the labor force for the tavern. The *Tennessee Gazetteer* of 1834 listed another tavern and two stores in Montgomery at that date, but noted only five or six families living in the town.

"Ye Olde Tavern," built about 1825 at Montgomery, was a log dogtrot structure later covered with clapboard. (Courtesy of Charles Kreis)

Growth of the County

Morgan County's population doubled between 1820 and 1850, from 1676 to 3430, but it was still sparsely populated compared with other counties in the state. The year 1850 was a high point in the county's population until 1880, when the population grew dramatically. Most of the residents between 1820 and 1850 were white. The economic status of the white population and the poor soil and climate for growing cotton and other crops suitable for slave labor accounted for the small black population. The 1820 census listed 46 slaves. The 1830 census showed 60 slaves in the county, and six free blacks, compared to 2516 whites. The Negro blacksmith in Montgomery, Robert Bush, owned his wife, Rebecca. He had paid $100 for her in 1843. In 1849 he petitioned the county court to set her free, a request that the court granted. Bush was concerned that his wife would be sold to someone else as a slave when he died.

The 1836 tax list showed 17 slaveowners in Morgan County, but the total number of slaves counted on the list was 36, so it must have been incomplete. The 1840 census showed 84 slaves. The value of these slaves was $400 to $600 per individual, although Moses Sexton listed one slave with a value of $1300. Edward Field owned the largest number of slaves—eight—with a total value of $4400, a considerable sum in 1836. Other owners claimed one to three slaves. In 1844 J. H. Schooler named ten slaves as his property in a deed of trust. Six of them were females, ranging in age from 3 to 50.

In 1860, five years before the abolition of slavery, Morgan County had 25 slaveholders with 120 slaves. Some of the owners were Reuben Davis, Edward Freels, Luke Hall, James Kelly, Thomas S. Lea, Collins Roberts, J. H. Schooler, Julian Scott, Thomas Scott, Thomas Staples, William Staples, Shadrack Stephens, Daniel Stonecipher, and Samuel Vaughn.

As was the case in other areas of the South, segregation was not characteristic in Morgan County before the Civil War. Housing was not segregated, and neither were public meetings. Union Baptist Church, organized in 1846, had black members who were addressed as "brother" and "sister," and who appear to have had equal rights with other members.

Agriculture dominated the fledgling economy of Morgan County. By the middle of the century there were 430 farms in the county producing a variety of products. The 1840 census reported over 53,000 bushels of "Indian corn," the English and early American words used to distinguish this grain from wheat, which was also called corn. This was by far the largest production of any type of grain, compared to 1261 bushels of wheat in the same year. Corn was usually the predominant crop of frontier economies in the United States. Tobacco and Irish potatoes were other early crops. Horses, mules, and oxen were important work animals, although oxen were not counted in the 1840 census. In the 1860 census 473 working oxen were counted, compared to 515 horses and 71 mules and asses. Swine, cattle, and sheep were important animals, and wool was a useful and profitable product. In 1840 the county produced 224 pounds of wool.

By 1860 the number of farms in the county dropped to 402, possibly accounted for by the exodus of settlers from Wartburg; but the totals of agricultural produce increased. Farmers harvested almost 110,000 bushels of corn, 8000 bushels of wheat,

12,000 bushels of sweet potatoes, and 13,000 bushels of Irish potatoes. The number of horses and mules, cattle, and swine declined, but the number of sheep increased. Molasses and wine were listed for the first time, with over 200 gallons of wine produced. The European settlers moving into the Wartburg area had brought the knowledge of grape growing and wine making with them.

The farms in Morgan County in the first half of the nineteenth century were relatively small compared to those in western Tennessee. In 1860 there were no farms in Morgan County with over 500 acres while West Tennessee counties listed many. Only 44 farms in Morgan County contained over 100 acres. Most of the farms, about half the total number in 1860, were 20 to 50 acres, although the average size of all farms in Tennessee in that census was 351 acres. The small size is explained by the hilly nature of Morgan County and by the relatively poor soil.

Industry definitely played a secondary part in the county's economy in the first half of the nineteenth century. The 1820 census listed leather, hides, hats, turpentine, maple sap, and whiskey as industrial products of the county. The term "industrial products" was used loosely because only three of the above were finished products; the others were raw materials. The census listed one tanyard in operation and one whiskey still producing 100 gallons. Total value of all these products in 1820 was $2102.

In 1840 there were two tanneries and two distilleries in the county. Two men worked in each of the industries, and about $3000 in capital was invested. This is very small in light of the fact that East Tennessee was the most highly industrialized section of the state at this time. By 1860 there was one tanyard, and no distilleries were listed. Two gristmills and three sawmills had been added, employing a total of ten men.

The main markets for Morgan County goods and purchases were Kingston, Knoxville, Chattanooga, and Nashville. Carts or wagons pulled by oxen, horses, or mules provided transportation. Nashville was generally considered too distant, thus the

The Isaac Laymance mill, with millstones brought from North Carolina, and home on Crooked Fork Creek. (Courtesy of Charles Kreis)

haul to markets there too expensive. Kingston, the closest market to Morgan County, was the most popular.

Coal, the backbone resource of Morgan County's economy, was first extracted as early as 1819. This operation was probably on Indian Creek, near Oliver Springs, in the extreme eastern edge of the county. John H. Kain reported that the miners sold the coal to forges in Knoxville. The first commercial shipments of coal in the state came from a mine on a fork of Poplar Creek. Henry H. Wiley hauled it four miles by wagon to Poplar Creek, loaded it on barges, took it down the creek to the Clinch River, then down the Tennessee River to Chattanooga, Huntsville, and Decatur. In 1860 there were two mines in operation in the county, employing nine men and representing an investment of $25,000. The value of the coal produced that year was $15,000.

Ostentatious wealth was not evident in Morgan County in the first half of the nineteenth century. The one man who owned almost 50 slaves was wealthy, for most Tennesseans owned no slaves, and only about one percent of the slaveowners had more than 50. But this man was not among the wealthiest citizens of the state in 1860. The "industrialists" and the mine owners were not even as wealthy as the slaveowner. An 1844 deed in Morgan County listed the household possessions of John H. Brient, operator of a stable in Montgomery and presumably a man of comfortable circumstances: 1 bed and furniture [mattress and bed hangings], 3 bedsteads, 1 bureau, 2 tables, 4 chairs, 1 candle stand, 1 trunk, 2 chests, 1 straw basket, 1 clock, 2 pairs of fire dogs, 1 pair of steelyards [balance scale], 1 oven, 1 pot, 1 skillet, 1 pair of fire tongs and shovel, 12 glass bottles and jars, 6 medical books, 1 history of the Revolution, 1 large map of the United States, 1 rifle and shot pouch. A meager inventory today, this probably represented as many of life's necessities as most inhabitants of Morgan County could boast at this time.

Morgan County's school system dates back to 1827, when Walden's Academy was chartered in Montgomery. In 1836 eight civil districts were created; there was to be one common school in each district. These areas were too large, so in 1848 the commissioners created smaller school districts. One school in the first district stood between Stoneciphers and Davis, and another common school operated in Montgomery. A board of common school commissioners directed the system.

A. B. Wright, who attended school in neighboring Fentress County, described his experience. The school terms varied from six weeks to three months, beginning in August. Additional time might be taken from school by the students for fodder pulling. Learning was in the form of recitations, and the teacher used a stick to prod memories and maintain discipline. Normally the instructor sat before the class with beech or hickory switch in hand during the recitation period, applying it in the presence of all the students when needed.

Some students attended Sunday school for academic instruction, and this may have been the only form of schooling for many children. Sunday school continued all day, unless there was preaching, prayer meeting, or class meeting that day. In addition to the Bible, students studied spelling books and readers to learn these basics.

A number of settlements and villages sprang up in Morgan

County in the first half of the nineteenth century to serve as meeting places and markets. The facts about their early histories are vague and indefinite.

Sunbright, Burrville, and Deer Lodge were early villages in the northern part of the county. The area around Sunbright was first settled by Benjamin T. Staples about 1814, by John Freels on White Oak Creek in 1811, and by Basil Human on Bone Camp. Louis Mosier was one of the early settlers who lived on the site of the town. The name "Sunbright" was only adopted in the 1870s with the coming of the railroad. When the post office opened in 1845, the town was called Pine Top. Later it was Stapleton after Tolliver Staples, one of its first settlers; then finally Sunbright. The first business building in the town may have been a boarding house owned and operated by Mosier.

Burrville, originally called Mt. Vernon, derived its name from the burrs of chestnut trees which flourished in the area. Six miles northwest of Sunbright, it was located near Clear Fork River. Both 1810 and 1830 have been given as founding dates for the village, but the latter is more likely. Settlers from North Carolina, Virginia, and Kentucky obtained grants of one thousand acres from Tennessee and settled this area. John Galloway and James Peters owned the land on which the community is now located. Other families in the immediate area were the Alexanders, Cromwells, Davises, Hulls, Hurts, Johnsons, Joneses, McCormicks, and Thorntons.

The first settler near Deer Lodge was a man named Grimes, who lived there about 1810. James Davidson, son of William L., bought about 300 acres in 1813. The Nashville-Knoxville Turnpike passed through this area, increasing the value of the land and the likelihood of settlement. Hack Hendrix operated a blacksmith shop on the turnpike about seven miles west of Deer Lodge. In 1845 James Davidson built and operated a grist- and sawmill powered by water. Another man named Bowmer operated a mill three miles west of Deer Lodge on Witt Creek. The town was known as Dead Level in 1870 when the first post office was established. Abner Ross, landowner and promoter of the town and area, supplied the present name in the 1880s after bringing deer from the Rugby area.

Lancing, along with the three county seats, occupies the center of Morgan County. Located on the Nashville-Knoxville Turnpike, it was settled in the 1860s. One of the first settlers was John White, and other early inhabitants were John Anderson, the Reverend Bordmen, Hillman Davidson, William Matthew Jones, Thomas Roberts, Fred Walt, and Dr. A. S. Wiltsy. Until the coming of the railroad in 1879 the town was called Kismet, but by 1894 Lancing was the accepted name at the insistence of railroad officials.

Coalfield, established about 1850, is the oldest settlement in the southeastern part of the county. Located on the Little Emory River, it was first settled by Shack Ruffner, who operated a water mill on the river for grinding grain. Known as Ruffner's Station, the settlement grew around the mill. Other early families were Adcock, Davis, Easter, Hudson, Jackson, Justice, Lyles, Stonecipher, and Woods. The first post office, established before the Civil War, was called Rio. Coalfield became the official name about 1900 when the coal mines began operating and shipping.

Other settlements established in Morgan County before the Civil War were Anderson's Cross Roads in 1833, Catoosa about 1840, and Pine Orchard. Anderson's was a post office set up as part of the policy of the Andrew Jackson administration. Many post offices established in 1833 were later discontinued. "Catoosa," a word which means "among these hills," was nestled at the foot of Crab Orchard Mountain in the southwestern part of the county. Pine Orchard, on Crab Orchard Creek, was settled by the Alley, Bingham, Hatfield, Headrick, Gallaher, Kittrell, Lively, McGell, McGuffey, Powell, Snow, Stout, Weatherford, and White families. Both a church and a school, Blake School, were established to serve the settlers.

Before the middle of the nineteenth century most of the settlers in Morgan County were Americans migrating from other parts of the country to this sparsely populated area. About 1850 the natural beauty of Morgan County and the ready availability of land attracted the attention of Europeans. A few Welsh settlers moved to the Huntsville (Scott County) area in the 1850s, the only success in a larger effort to establish Welsh settlements in Morgan County. Englishmen attempted to settle the northern part of the county, around Rugby, but they were unsuccessful. Polish miners and mill workers helped to populate the Deer Lodge area about 1890, but most of them actually came from other parts of the United States.

The most successful incursion of Europeans into Morgan County was the German and Swiss colonization of the Wartburg area in the middle of the county in the 1840s and 1850s. These settlers were part of a large body of Germans seeking to escape from the poor economic conditions in their homeland. Between 1830 and 1850 almost 600,000 Germans moved into the United States, their favorite choice for a new home and a new hope.

In 1828 Traugott Bromme, a German traveler, passed through Tennessee. He visited Roane, Anderson, and Morgan counties, then painted a favorable picture of the area in a book published in 1834. Bromme's book circulated widely among Germans in the northern part of the United States, and several German businessmen there began to investigate investment opportunities in Tennessee. George F. Gerding of New York was one of the first to act. In 1843 Gerding bought some of this land from Henry Wells, one of the original purchasers. Gerding had never seen East Tennessee, but he was impressed by reports of its climate, timber, pasture lands, and mineral wealth. He assumed that the prospects for sheep raising and for development of iron and coal resources were bright. In 1844 he organized the East Tennessee Colonization Company, in partnership with Theodore de Cock of Antwerp and five other directors from Europe and New York. The chief assets of the company consisted of more than 170,000 acres of land in the modern counties of Morgan, Cumberland, White, Fentress and Scott. This was to be the only German colonization attempt in Tennessee prior to 1860. Most of the German colonies were established in the Midwest.

Friedrich R. Guenther, an employee of the Gerding business in New York, was resident agent of the East Tennessee Colonization Company. He located in Morgan County to conduct the business of the company there, selling land and receiving settlers. In 1844 he left New York for Morgan County, where he met John White, a native of the county who assisted him in establishing the colony.

In the meantime the directors of the company and a number of employed agents began to seek buyers and settlers for the East Tennessee Land Company project. The greatest efforts were made in the German state of Saxony, where economic distress had been severe, though efforts were also made in the Rhineland, Baden, and Switzerland. Gerding recruited after he was appointed U.S. consul for Baden in 1845. In the United States, agents in New York, New Orleans, and Charleston were on the docks to greet arriving immigrants and recruit them for the East Tennessee Land Company. Gerding operated a packet ship line from Antwerp to New York in partnership with J. C. Kunckelmann. The four sailing vessels of this line were convenient transports for persons moving from Europe to the Tennessee colony.

In 1845 the efforts resulted in the first 50 settlers for the project. Recruited in Mainz, Germany, this group of about 15 families sailed to the port of New Orleans, arriving in the middle of the summer. Traveling up the Mississippi and Cumberland rivers by steamboat, the immigrants were repeatedly approached by agents of other land companies. At Nashville, Friedrick Guenther and John White greeted the group.

This first group of settlers impressed the citizens of Nashville. The *Nashville Whig* reported that "two or three hundred immigrants are daily expected to arrive," and when the first 50 did arrive, the paper observed that "the immigrants are far superior to the general run of that description of persons . . . none but individuals with good character and habits will be permitted to join the colony."

White and Guenther guided the settlers, in ox carts, through Middle Tennessee and over the Cumberland Plateau on the Nashville-Knoxville Turnpike. The travelers must have been impressed by the natural beauty of the area, but they may have been concerned by the sparsity of human habitation and by the very different culture. Arriving on the site of Wartburg in Morgan County, the immigrants were severely disappointed.

Guenther and White had tried to make some preparation for the settlers. The streets of the new town had been platted and named, but they were not formed or even cleared. A "receiving house" had been built to shelter new arrivals. It was a two-story log structure, some 70 or 90 feet by 30 feet. Each floor had three rooms, and each room had two windows, one on the front side and one on the back. Each floor had a porch in front. There were no fireplaces or stoves in the building when the first settlers arrived, so they had to cook outside over open fires. Later, stoves with pipes were installed for heat and cooking. The receiving house was not large enough to accommodate all the first arrivals, so the lucky ones were housed at Scott's Tavern in Montgomery, about a mile away. A storehouse with office for the agent had also been built, operated by John White in conjunction with Guenther, the agent.

The land company assumed that the first settlers would engage in agriculture, so the company purchased and shipped to Morgan County some Saxony rams to promote sheep raising and production of wool. The company also suggested cultivating vineyards and orchards. Considering the climate and geography of Morgan County, the settlers would have been wise to have followed this advice; but many attempted crops for which the area was not suited.

The site for the new town of Wartburg was on the Nashville-Knoxville Turnpike at the southwest end of Bird Mountain, where the turnpike began its abrupt descent to the Emory River. The town was named "Wartburg" after the castle in Thuringia, Germany, where Martin Luther translated the Bible into German. Pastor Friedrich Behr described his new home as "the paradise of North America, . . . a region resembing . . . the forests of Thuringia." Wartburg's establishment provided a focus for settlement in the county, and the town became a market place, political hub, and social center for the area.

The plat for Wartburg showed six streets running north and south, each 60 feet wide and each named with a Roman numeral

"I" through "VI." The east-west streets, also 60 feet wide, crossed the north-south streets to form 240-foot squares. The east-west streets were named for European cities, with the main thoroughfare dubbed "Antwerp." Each square was divided into six lots to be sold, and a public square was designated between Antwerp and Cologne streets. Trees were to be planted along two streets and on the public square. These ambitious plans were unrealized for some time, and as late as 1848 all of the streets except Antwerp remained uncleared and unformed.

In 1845 Guenther proposed to move the county seat from Montgomery to Wartburg. As encouragement for the county to accept this company offer, Guenther offered to erect a courthouse and jail on the public square in Wartburg without expense to the county. He pledged "neat and commodious buildings"; nevertheless, his proposal was rejected by the Montgomery government.

Town lots in Wartburg sold for $10 to $30, a reasonable price. Small tracts of land near town were $3 to $15 an acre, and large tracts sold for $.50 to $4 an acre. Company directors instructed Guenther to employ the first settlers in constructing buildings and houses on the town lots. Evidently misunderstanding these directions, Guenther foolishly employed them building a fence around 400 acres of timberland, costing the company $1300 and delaying the development of Wartburg. Then the first settlers spread into the countryside to prepare their farms for cultivation and to erect log houses. Most of the immigrants had arranged to purchase their farms before they left Mainz, and they were anxious to clear and develop the land. Unfortunately, they soon ran out of money and provisions, and unfavorable weather conditions in the autumn and winter further discouraged them.

In 1846 the fortunes of the new colony appeared to improve. Two contingents of settlers arrived, one in March of 1846 and another in September. Wartburg appeared more hospitable than it had the year before. Some of the streets in the town were laid out, and the roads to the town were improved. Haag Tavern, owned by the land company and kept by Carl Haag in a two-story frame building, provided entertainment and refreshment for the residents and new arrivals. John F. Wilken, Lutheran minister, initiated worship services and opened a school for the spiritual and intellectual nourishment of the settlers. A Dr. Brandau, employed by the company for $250 annual subsidy, opened an office in Haag Tavern to handle the medical needs of the populace.

Most of the European immigrants who settled in the Wartburg colony arrived between 1846 and 1855, and most were from Germany or Switzerland. There is no total available for the number of immigrants. Gerding used the number 2000, H. S. Cooper (in a University of Tennessee thesis) estimated 800–1000, and the 1850 census reported 317 foreign-born persons in the Wartburg area.

Despite the foreign origin of the inhabitants, Gerding anglicized Wartburg in 1847 by changing the names of the streets. The east-west streets became Rose, Church, Maidenland, Kingston, Mill, and Cumberland. The north-south streets were Eliza, Court, Main, Spring, and Green. In 1851 the town was incorporated.

Most of the settlers lived on land outside the town. They purchased 15,000 to 20,000 acres from the East Tennessee Land Company, mostly south and west of Wartburg. There was little settlement north of town. Some small tracts, from 2 to 30 acres, were close to town along New Kingston Road South. Along the turnpike road east there were tracts up to 75 acres. The largest farms were south of Wartburg. The Forstner and Freytag tracts exceeded 1000 acres. In the Melhorn settlement southwest of town and on the west side of the Emory River, C. F. Melhorn owned 1356 acres. In the Sona settlement were other large tracts. Four persons in the Wartburg colony owned more than 1000 acres and six owned 350 to 1000 acres.

In 1847 additional troubles plagued the new colony. Guenther was replaced as resident agent for the colony because the directors were disappointed by lack of profit from the land company. Guenther had made some mistakes which cost the company money, but he was an amiable and honest man whom the colonists liked and trusted. The people neither liked nor

Old Engert log house with cantilevered second story and partially enclosed dogtrot. (Courtesy of Charles Kreis)

trusted Otto von Kienbusch, Guenther's successor. He was a better businessman than Guenther, and the settlers thought he sought to make profit for the company by demanding exaggerated prices for land. In 1849 Gerding dismissed Kienbusch and moved to Wartburg with his family to direct the colony himself and act as resident agent for the land company. Gerding's presence inspired confidence in the settlers, and he was lovingly dubbed "Little Dutch King" by the residents of his colony.

In addition to the price of the land, other complaints concerned the condition of the land and its lack of productivity. Some of the Swiss settlers in the colony complained that they had purchased farms described as "estates," but they arrived in Morgan County to discover only undeveloped wilderness. The early farmers also complained about crop failures, the blame for which could have been laid to the farmers' unfamiliarity with the climate and the soil.

A decrease in the number of immigrants was another problem that the colony encountered. After 1848 no large groups arrived in Wartburg, and some settlers left because of the problems noted above.

Even the church in Wartburg was part of the troubles of the time. John Wilken, an employee of the land company, served as pastor to all the settlers in the colony. Wilken was a Lutheran, as were many of the settlers. Some were Swiss Reformed, however, and when Wilken refused to preach or serve communion according to the Reform creed, they split from the church and stormed the pastor's house armed with pitchforks. The church council supported Wilken and prevented his dismissal by the company. The Swiss Reformed created a separate congregation and worshipped in the home of Johann Kreis.

By 1850 the colony was struggling for survival. More residents departed from Wartburg than arrived, the dissatisfied moving to Knoxville, Kingston, Rockwood, or Nashville to seek jobs and a better life. The California gold rush of 1848 also called some young men away from Morgan County. A German writer, Johann C. Buttner, passed through Wartburg about 1850. He sounded the death knell for the colony in his handbook for foreign travelers:

> The settlement does not prosper and it will most likely be abandoned as a colony. The land is too poor, the roads are too bad and the journey required to reach it is too costly and too troublesome in relation to what one finds there.

In 1849 the Wartburg colony's population was about 475. Few colonists lived in town because the land agents had concentrated on selling farms rather than town lots and because the town lots were overpriced compared to the farm land. Gerding lived in a rather pleasant house which contained his store. A clerk lived with him. There was a building serving as a church and school house. Haag's Tavern housed his family of five persons as well as his business and Dr. Brandau's office. Widow Bauerdeller lived in a log cabin, and Pastor Wilken's frame house was beside the cabin. Dr. Kramer, with his wife and four children, lived with the pastor. Mr. von Kienbusch was still living in Wartburg in a log

Swiss Reformed Church, Wartburg, was built in 1856. (Courtesy of Charles Kreis)

cabin, although he was no longer the land company agent. John White, with his wife, seven children, and a slave, lived in a nice frame house next to the market square. The receiving house still existed and was in use at this time. One observer commented that the town "considerably dampens the expectations."

Wartburg was a center of activity, despite the fact that few lived in town. The Lutheran church was located there, and since most of the German settlers were of that denomination, they presumably traveled regularly to Wartburg for services. The Reverend Wilken and his congregation completed a new church in 1855. The Swiss Reformed group of fifty families led by the Reverend Johann Etter built a church in 1856. Etter traveled for more than a year in 1854 and 1855, in both the northern part of the United States and in Switzerland, to collect funds with which to build the structure.

A school opened in the Luthern church in Wartburg. In the beginning Wilken conducted this school, with instruction offered in both German and English. Etter and his wife also taught a school for children of the Swiss Reformed church in the 1850s.

Social activities of the German-Swiss colony must also have centered in Wartburg, with its churches and its taverns. The afternoon social occasion of *Kaffeetrinken* was a customary activity of the ladies. They gathered in a home for coffee or tea, cake, and conversation. Weddings lasted as long as a week, consisting of food, drink, gifts, and dancing. People made Dutch punch with American corn whiskey, and drank homemade grape and fruit wines. They celebrated Christmas as a festival centering around churches. The Gemans observed five days of religious ceremony, then several more days for dancing and feasting.

Wartburg had an unusually large number of professionally trained individuals. There was one architect, Carl Rothe, with a degree from Leipzig University. He aided in the construction of some modest structures in the colony before moving to Knoxville for better opportunities. A professional musician, Gustav Knabe, also a Leipzig University graduate, lived in Wartburg for some time before accepting a position on the Maryville College faculty. Eight physicians practiced in or near Wartburg during the 1850s, an unusually large number for such a small population. The land company had brought in two medical doctors, Brandau and Edward Goetz. Goetz, a native of Baden in Germany, had been recruited by Gerding in Mannheim. Dr. F. A. Sienknecht came to the colony in 1848 from his native Holstein. He bought a small tract of land and opened a drug store in Wartburg, growing herbs and preparing many of his own medicines. Dr. Rudolf Knaffl, a New York physician born in Vienna, bought land in Morgan County and moved there to improve his failing health. He practiced medicine while living in semiretirement. Dr. Charles F. Kramer, born in England, lived in Wartburg and played an active role in the colony. He was on the first board of commissioners for the town. Dr. Christian Rauschenberg, from Leipzig, lived in the colony from 1847 to 1849, practicing medicine and exploring the area with his brother-in-law, Alexander Gerhardt of the Zoological Museum of Leipzig. Dr. Johannes Majorsky was in the colony in 1847. Dr. Sienknecht was the most constant of these physicians, working in the area until 1883.

One German noble, Baron F. von Forstner of Stuttgart, moved to Morgan County with his wife, two sons, and three daughters after a colonization attempt in Texas collapsed. Von Forstner bought 1500 acres in Morgan County and built a large home on it. Despite his concern about the remoteness of Morgan County, he lived there until his death in 1860.

Skilled craftsmen were numerous in and around Wartburg. Johann Kreis formed a construction company in 1846 and built many of the substantial structures in the colony. The residences he constructed were two-story with clapboard siding and clay-straw insulation. Stone chimneys and interiors with hand-dressed material distinguished his work. The Wartburg Piano Company was the most unusual of the craft industries. Gerding's oldest son and Fritz Beneike, both of whom built pianos in New York, moved to Wartburg and opened such a firm there. They employed Heinrich Waltersdorf, also a pianomaker from New York. The men produced several pianos, purchasing material from a Philadelphia company. For some time the piano business was quite profitable. Furniture making was a craft of Johann A. Aurin, who brought his sons to Wartburg and employed several other workers in a furniture factory. Cabinetmakers were numerous in the colony. Otto von Kienbusch and Gustav Brandau opened a tobacco firm in Montgomery. They made cigars and smoking tobacco from the crops grown in Morgan County, marketing their products in Knoxville, Nashville, and Cincinnati. Other craftsmen and laborers in Wartburg in 1850 included painter, cooper, blacksmith, stonemason, wagonmaker, tinner, weaver, shoemaker, tanner, bookbinder, and silversmith.

A number of mills operated in and around Wartburg. John White owned a grist- and sawmill on Crooked Fork Creek, and Gerding had a gristmill, a flour mill, and an oil mill (probably turpentine) on the same creek, run by Jakob Kreis. As early as 1846 Johann Kreis and Christian Kreis operated the first sawmill on the Emory River west of Wartburg. Melhorn Mill, Kuhn Mill, and Nitzschke Mill were also a part of the industrial scene around Wartburg.

Agriculture remained the major economic enterprise in the colony. The first crops were failures, and stockraising was unsuccessful at first because of no market. Sheep, cattle, and even poultry were not produced on a commercial scale; only a few flocks of geese were marketed annually in Knoxville. In the 1850s it was even difficult to obtain meat in Wartburg at times. The 1850 census listed a butcher in the town, but he evidently was gone by the middle of the decade; the nearest butcher was then in Knoxville. Milk was not sold on a commercial basis outside the colony before the Civil War. Only after the Civil War did Joseph Gschwend and others raise cattle to market in Knoxville and Cincinnati.

One successful agricultural enterprise in Morgan County that was new for Tennessee was grape growing and the companion activity of wine making. Several large vineyards, as well as a number of orchards, were planted. Brandies were produced, but wine was the biggest commercial success. The climate and soil in Morgan County favored grape growing, and the Swiss and German settlers had the necessary knowledge to cultivate the vines and produce the wine. The *Kingston Gazetteer* claimed that Wartburg wine would "compare well with those manufactured in Europe." The 1860 census reported 242 gallons produced in Morgan County, and it sold for the favorable price of four dollars a gallon.

Tobacco soon became a cash crop in Morgan County, as it was in much of the southeast. The settlers were not familiar with the cultivation of this weed when they settled in Tennessee, but by 1850 Morgan County produced 6735 pounds for the market and for the tobacco factory in Montgomery.

The largest farms in the colony generally belonged to the German settlers. Another group that owned small acreage but engaged wholly in agriculture was the vintners, who usually cultivated orchards as well as vineyards. Joseph Falwinchl, David Kuhn, Richard Ritz, G. J. Mersch, and Johann Liencenwanger were names associated with grape culture. Swiss settlers tended to own small plots of land and farm part-time,while plying a craft or trade in or near Wartburg.

The agricultural economy of Wartburg and Morgan County operated largely on the subsistence level before the Civil War. No large markets were close, and transportation was so poor that produce could not be moved out of the county to the distant markets. The industrial economy was stifled for the same reasons. Those who wanted to deal on a commercial basis tended to become discouraged by the conditions. Many became so disheartened by the primitive economy that they moved to near or distant cities to ply their trade.

Two other plans to settle Germans in colonies in Morgan County failed completely. By 1870 there were only 57 German-born and 41 Swiss-born residents in the entire county. Wartburg, the center of the German-Swiss colony, became the county seat in 1870; it became the administrative center for the entire area and lost its significance as a German-Swiss center.

State and National Politics

In the 1830s Morgan County citizens took part in state and national politics. They normally agreed with and expressed the same attitudes as other counties in East Tennessee, even though they were somewhat isolated and even though the county had some European population after 1845.

In 1833 Tennessee voted to revise its constitution to make it more democratic. Voters approved the convention by more than 8000 votes. Morgan County was even more enthusiastic than the state as a whole, voting 284 for and only 21 opposing. Sixty delegates from across the state convened in Nashville in May of 1834. John Whitson represented Morgan and Anderson counties.

The new constitution, with a significantly more democratic flavor for whites than the constitution of 1796, was put to the voters for ratification. In March of 1835 Tennesseans accepted the document by a vote of 42,666 to 17,691. Morgan County voters enthusiastically approved the new constitution, voting 230 for and 19 against.

In gubernatorial elections Morgan County was not constant in its adherence to either the Whig or the Democratic party. East Tennessee had a strong Whig tradition, but Morgan County on its western edge did not consistently comply with this trend. In 1861 the county was so strongly in favor of Tennessee remaining in the Union that it chose William H. Polk over Isham G. Harris 489 to 43, after favoring Harris very strongly in two earlier elections. Voters changed parties and supported or rejected individual candidates according to the issues of the particular time.

In presidential elections Morgan County was just as inconsistent in its party loyalty. Some pattern to the voting was indicated in that the county voted for Democrats when the candidate was a Tennessean. In 1832 Andrew Jackson was the overwhelming choice of the county, which gave him 108 votes to 8 for Whig Henry Clay of Kentucky. Likewise, in 1844, Democrat and Tennessean James K. Polk received 232 votes to 211 for Clay. Polk was not so popular in the county at this time, which had voted against him for governor in 1841; but he was a Tennessean. In other elections before 1850 the county usually voted Whig, as was the East Tennessee tradition. In the two other elections before the war the county went Democrat, voting for James Buchanan in 1856 and John C. Breckinridge in 1860. Considering the voting history and the attitudes of the county, one might have suspected that John Bell of Tennessee would have carried Morgan in 1860. Bell represented the Constitutional Union Party and the principles of Morgan County. In addition he was a native son. Bell, who carried the state, did receive 168 votes in the county to 218 for Breckinridge. The other Democrat, Stephen Douglas, gathered only 46 votes with his popular sovereignty principle. Abraham Lincoln and the Republican Party received no votes in Morgan County. After the Civil War the county did consistently vote Republican.

East Tennessee expressed the earliest and most vocal antislavery sentiment in the state. Governor Harris, however, delivered a proslavery and pro-South speech to a special session of the legislature in January of 1861. South Carolina had already seceded from the Union, and Governor Harris asked the legislature to call a referendum to determine if the voters wanted a secession convention. The referendum was set for February of 1861, and by a substantial margin the voters said "no convention," with only West Tennessee voting for a secession convention. Morgan County voted overwhelmingly against the convention–488 to 13.

By the first of February, Georgia, Florida, Alabama, Mississippi, Louisiana, and Texas had followed South Carolina in seceding from the Union. In that month six of these states met in Montgomery, Alabama, and created the Confederate States of America. In April the Confederates fired the first shots of the Civil War and captured Fort Sumter in Charleston harbor. When President Lincoln asked Tennessee for troops to suppress rebellion in South Carolina, Governor Harris responded, "Tennessee will not furnish a single man." He called a special session of the legislature and recommended secession. The General Assembly declared independence and secession on May 6, and called for a referendum to ratify secession on June 8.

East Tennessee, still opposed to secession, held its own convention in Knoxville in May of 1861. T. A. R. Nelson, a prominent East Tennessean and Union man, presided. Morgan County sent six delegates: S. C. Honeycutt, E. Langley, J. M. Melton, B. T. Staples, M. Stephens, and Jesse Stonecipher. This meeting expressed strong pro–Union sentiments.

After the convention in Knoxville, and before the state referendum to ratify secession, Nelson and Andrew Johnson toured East Tennessee to rally Union support. They addressed more than two thousand people in Clinton, and in the next few days they spoke in Jacksboro, Huntsville, and Jamestown. Two days before the referendum they were in Montgomery, Morgan's county seat, for a last-minute rally; then on to Kingston for a final speech on the eve of the referendum.

On voting day, June 8, Tennessee accepted secession by a substantial margin. Middle Tennesseeans had changed their minds after the fight at Fort Sumter; only East Tennessee was still pro–Union. More than 104,000 Tennesseans voted to secede from the United States and join the Confederate States; only 47,238 opposed secession and favored the Union. East Tennesseans voted 14,780 for secession, and 32,923 for remaining in the Union. Morgan County joined with all the counties around her to oppose secession, voting 630 against and only 50 for separation.

On June 17, 1861, East Tennesseans convened for a four-day meeting in Greeneville to consider the state's decision to leave the Union. T. A. R. Nelson again presided. All East Tennessee counties except Rhea were represented. Morgan County sent six delegates: T. H. Davis, S. C. Honeycutt, W. R. Jackson, E. Langley, J. M. Melton, and Jesse Stonecipher. The men at this convention concluded that the state's decision to separate from the Union was not binding on citizens, and they talked about separating from Tennessee, though only Scott County did attempt to do so.

While Morgan County was substantially pro-Union, this sentiment was not unanimous. The founder of Wartburg, George Gerding, was strongly secessionist and pro-Confederate. He left Wartburg for the duration of the war, sitting out the conflict in Louisville, Kentucky. Carl Aurin, Rudolf Braun, and Rudolf Freytag also supported the Confederate states during the war. On the other hand, Drs. Edward Goetz and Gustav Brandau served as medical officers in the United States Army during the war. Dr. F. A. Sienknecht supported the Union, but two of his sons joined the Confederate army. The congregations of the German and Swiss churches in Wartburg split over the war, with the Reverend Wilken strongly supporting the Union. O. G. von Kienbusch, a Union sympathizer, was forced to flee Morgan County for his safety, and Pastor Wilken departed until the area was in Union hands.

Civil War (by Dr. Larry H. Whiteaker)

As the war began, resistance to the Confederacy produced a dilemma for the Morgan County Unionists. Kentucky beckoned them as a Union haven. There they could reside in relative safety until the war's conclusion, or the men could attempt to undermine the Confederacy in a more direct way by joining the Union army. By the summer of 1861, Unionists from several Tennessee counties, including Morgan, were gathering at Camp Dick Robinson and other Union outposts in Kentucky to offer their services.

Flight to Union lines was not an easy decision to make. Service with the Union meant leaving families, farms, and businesses behind to an uncertain fate. If the men tried to remain in Morgan County, they placed their own lives in peril. With Confederate authority increasing throughout the state, neither Unionists nor their property were safe. It is no wonder that Morgan Countians, regardless of political sympathies, tended to view the war with great foreboding. Morgan County was about to endure four terrible years.

As the county residents struggled with their loyalty dilemmas, Confederate authorities implemented military plans that soon affected these decisions. The county's geographical position assumed great strategic importance in maintaining Confederate transportation and communication lines through East Tennessee and in keeping the region's farms a "breadbasket" for the South. As one of the gateways to East Tennessee, Morgan County had to be kept in Confederate hands.

A Union invasion of East Tennessee, Confederate military officers reported, would likely come on one of three routes. The Cumberland Gap was the best known and was perhaps the easiest for an army to use, but a more westerly route from Williamsburg, Kentucky, to Jacksboro was a possibility too. The third road was even farther west, running from Monticello, Kentucky, through Jamestown to Morgan County itself. To protect the county and East Tennessee, the Confederates not only had to guard the roads, but also had to suppress Unionism among the residents.

In August of 1861 Confederate troops began securing the county and the surrounding area. From Livingston in Overton County, Second Tennessee Cavalry troops marched east to Jamestown and then on to Montgomery. Meeting no resistance, the soldiers continued on through Wartburg and finally stopped at Camp Schuyler, a Confederate post about four miles east of the town.

The Confederate forces found most of the county's male population absent. Dozens of Unionists had already fled to friendly territory, and news of the approaching troops forced others to do likewise. For those who determined to remain, the wooded hills provided the only safety. Hidden in the forests, provided with food and clothing by their families and friends, the Union men dared not emerge unless protected by the cover of darkness. They depended on a variety of signals—the blast of a horn, a ringing bell, a gunshot—to warn one another of approaching Confederates. Discovery, they soon learned, meant instant arrest and perhaps imprisonment. Even a male suspected of preparing to flee to Union lines could expect this harsh treatment.

By the early autumn of 1861, General Felix K. Zollicoffer, the Confederate commander in East Tennessee, had arranged his forces to protect not only the three invasion routes, but to provide a defensive arc for most of the region. This dispersed position of Zollicoffer's troops, it seems, freed Morgan County temporarily from military control. Although soldiers still traveled through the county and occasionally made use of Camp Schuyler, several months passed before the county drew attention again.

With the region supposedly secured, local Confederates, aided sometimes by "neutrals," made determined efforts to keep the county government functioning. In any area torn by civil war, divided loyalties often make social institutions the first casualties. Church congregations split, government officials lose authority, schools close, public services are suspended, and law and order disappear. The county Confederates could not prevent all this deterioration of the social fabric, but they could, with help from state authorities, stop some of it.

The county court continued to hold sessions in 1861 and on into 1862. In January, Confederate pressure played a role in having the county court elect James R. Stanfield sheriff. Stanfield subsequently became the first county officer to take the oath to support the Confederate constitution. Despite this avowal of loyalty, the sheriff and other local Confederates must have remained uneasy, knowing as they did that they were greatly outnumbered and that only the threat of military force restrained the Unionists.

By the early spring of 1862, Unionist opposition had reasserted itself to such a degree that an open challenge to Confederate authority was being made in the county. To quell this disloyalty, Confederate officials in late March sent an expedition into Unionist strongholds in both Morgan and Scott counties. On March 28, near Montgomery, the Confederate troops clashed with the local Union men. After thirty minutes of fighting, the Unionists withdrew, leaving behind some fifteen dead and several more wounded. The tragic outcome of this skirmish proved what many Unionists had already begun to suspect: relief from Confederate occupation would not come until a Union army invaded East Tennessee.

Morgan Countians, meanwhile, struggled simply for survival. By the second half of 1862, the county government had folded and the authority to maintain law and order had been replaced by the authority of the gun. Even Confederate law brought small comfort to Union sympathizers. Confederate confiscation policies permitted the taking of all foodstuffs and other supplies that the military needed, with payment considerably below the market price. Foraging parties became the bane of county farmers, as they took pigs, chickens, cows, wheat, and garden vegetables. Men hiding in the hills began to take their farm animals and produce with them.

Supplies from outside the county became difficult to obtain. The whole Confederacy suffered from an inflation-ridden economy and from shortages brought on in part by the Union blockade of Southern ports. Imported commodities such as coffee and sugar became scarce. Salt was a luxury. Families had to produce their own cloth and leather or do without new clothes and shoes.

These daily hardships would have been burdensome enough by themselves, but added to them was the horror of personal violence. Marauding bands of outlaws ("bushwhackers") began to plague the region, stealing, robbing, and murdering those who opposed them. More violence came from organized guerrilla forces, especially those led by the Unionist "Tinker Dave" Beatty of Fentress County or those headed by Champ Ferguson, a notorious Confederate guerrilla from White County. Regardless of which side they were on—or whether they were on any side at all—the marauders and guerrillas brought terrorism to all Morgan Countians.

Almost every family suffered during the war. Horror tales have survived through oral tradition, revealing how traumatic the times were. Craven Duncan, who was pressed for information about hidden Unionists, was stripped down to his underwear and forced by Confederate soldiers to stand outside in freezing weather, a form of torture that ruined his health. Rebecca Duncan watched her mother plead with soldiers not to take the family cow, only to hear them jeer at her and kill the cow in front of the family. On another occasion Confederates murdered Unionist Sim Lavender when he objected to their horses being driven into his cornfield.

As those woes continued, the Union army in the early summer of 1863 implemented its invasion plans for East Tennessee. In June, Colonel William P. Sanders and 1500 Union Cavalry troops from Kentucky made a spectacular raid into the region. By the 17th Sanders and his men had penetrated all the way to Montgomery. There Unionists told them about a small Confederate force in Wartburg. Surprising the rebels, Sanders' troops captured 104 soldiers and confiscated horses, food, and other supplies. As Sanders continued his raid deeper into East Tennessee, all Unionists knew that rescue from the Confederacy was soon to come.

In mid-August the invasion began. General Ambrose Burnside's Army of the Ohio, some 24,000 strong, left its base in Kentucky and proceeded across the mountains toward Knoxville, its main objective. By August 30, the army's advance units had entered Montgomery. Burnside and the main body of the soldiers arrived the following day. Unionist W. L. Davidson's home became the general's headquarters.

Having rested in Morgan County, Burnside's troops resumed their march toward Knoxville. Confederate skirmishers clashed with the advanced parties, but gave no ground. The outnumbered Confederate force in Knoxville abandoned the city. On September 3, Burnside entered Knoxville. The East Tennessee Unionists had been delivered.

For Morgan County Unionists, Burnside's invasion brought relief for some of their woes, but not all. No longer did the men have to worry about the Confederate draft law or harassment from Confederate officials. For the most part, they felt secure enough to leave their hideouts and resume ordinary life, but many hardships and dangers still confronted them. The economic problems continued, and with the lack of seed, farm tools, and labor, poor crops caused malnourishment throughout the county. To alleviate this, the Union authorities ordered rations to be given to people in the Cumberland Plateau area.

The danger of personal violence also lingered. The marauders ignored Union authority as much as they had ignored the Confederate, and the county's Confederate sympathizers received the same harassment from the Union soldiers that their side had imposed upon the Unionists. Guerrilla raids, moreover, still terrorized the county, particularly those by the Confederate Champ Ferguson.

On one occasion Ferguson and some of his men dressed themselves as Union soldiers and slipped into Morgan County to observe the enemy. Ferguson extracted information from D. S. Lavender, identified him as a Union man, and proceeded to Wartburg to spy on the Yankee guards. The next day, Ferguson attacked in force and captured the detachment. In the process of withdrawing, the guerrillas rode by Lavender's place and murdered him in his yard.

By the autumn of 1864, Union control over the region had so improved that Morgan Countians reinstituted their civilian government. The county court resumed its sessions and county officers began carrying out their duties by taking an oath of allegiance to the United States. In November county citizens voted in the presidential election.

Reconstruction

Morgan County was not physically devastated by the Civil War, as were some other parts of Tennessee where large and destructive battles occurred. Nevertheless, Morgan County suffered some effects from the conflict, as did so many other parts of the South. The population of the county actually declined between 1860 and 1870, from 3353 to 2969, and the war is the most logical explanation for the decline. Morgan County lost some soldiers on both sides in the war, and the county lost some civilians in the conflict. Other persons left the county during the war, never to return. Ten of the twenty-two charter members of the First Evangelical Lutheran Church in Knoxville in 1869 were former residents of Wartburg.

The black population of Morgan County declined disproportionately after the war, from 161 in 1860 to 101 by 1870, a decline of more than one-third. The small number of blacks in the county were now segregated for the first time. In 1874 there were one "colored" and 19 white schools in the county; there were no black teachers. The religious census of 1890 showed three Baptist Colored churches and six Colored Methodist Episcopal churches. Despite the coming of segregation, the county was not plagued by the Ku Klux Klan.

The area did suffer from smallpox and typhoid plagues after the war. Both diseases were rampant in the region for the remainder of the nineteenth century. Some individual cases may have developed earlier, but in the summer of 1881 a typhoid epidemic gripped the settlement at Rugby. Seven lost their lives. In 1882 smallpox broke out in the Annadel area. A special smallpox hospital was set up, and the county employed Dr. A. S. Wiltsie to attend the hospital for 40 days. R. E. Roxmyer acted as nurse, and two guards enforced the quarantine of the hospital. This operation cost the county more than $600 for the personnel, the rented house used as a hospital, vaccine and other supplies, and food for the patients.

The county government suffered from the war. In 1865 the justices in Montgomery declared that all proceedings and actions of the court between 1861 and 1865 were illegal and void; thus the county could not legally collect taxes during that period. In 1865 the county trustee, Jesse Stonecipher, refunded to taxpayers all monies collected in 1862, evidently the last year taxes were collected. So the county was bankrupt in 1865. At least old debts were gone, too, for the court declared that all warrants issued by the county during the war were illegal and therefore void.

Poverty was a significant problem in Morgan County after the Civil War. The county had always made some provision for orphans through the practice of binding and for paupers through money and provisions given them. In 1871, however, a more organized effort to deal with poverty was initiated. Commissioners for the poor were appointed, and the county purchased 200 acres near Deer Lodge from William Howard for use as a poor farm. This institution operated until 1899, when there was only one inmate and the county ordered the house sold.

Other residents of Morgan County were not living in high style after the war. Joseph B. Killebrew reported that there were only a few brick houses in the county and a larger number of frame. Many, he said, were made of hewn logs, which were the cheapest material. A. B. Wright confirmed Killebrew's survey. He described houses on the Cumberland Plateau after the Civil War as built of logs, chinked and daubed. He indicated that they were heated with fireplaces and that cooking was also done over the fire. Cooking stoves were rare in the area.

The famous naturalist John Muir passed through Fentress, Morgan, and Roane counties in 1867, traveling the road between Jamestown, Montgomery, and Kingston. He described Jamestown as a "poor, rickety, thrice-dead village, . . . an incredibly dreary place." Montgomery was "shabby." He observed empty houses and abandoned farms left from the war, and at one place between Jamestown and Montgomery the "road became dim and at last vanished among desolate fields." His description of the residents and their habitations indicated poverty. Two families with whom he tried to board could not change a five dollar bill.

Lawlessness resulting from the conditions of war was evident. Muir was warned numerous times about bandits and guerrillas. One young man on a horse tried to rob him, but discovered Muir had nothing of value. A gang of ten men with long hair and mounted on "scrawny" horses confronted him, but they also realized that he carried nothing of value to them.

Aside from the people, Muir thought the natural beauty of the area created the "most heavenly place I ever entered."

New County Seat

As the second half of the nineteenth century aproached its midway point, renewed life and progress could be observed in Morgan County as well as the entire state. The Civil War was becoming history, and the people of Tennessee and the South were looking forward, hoping and preparing for better times.

One of the first changes in Morgan County after the war was the relocation of the county seat. Wartburg had become an American town rather than a German settlement. The 1870 census showed only 98 German and Swiss people in the entire county, and the Reverend A. B. Wright thought the Germans were some of the "best people in the country . . . who spoke English plainly." The Lutheran church in Wartburg remained one last center of the German language and culture.

Symbolic of Wartburg's integration into the county, and symbolic of its importance to the county, was the relocation of the county seat in 1870. In 1865 talk about moving was heard. Montgomery had a population of about 50 and was declining, overshadowed both geographically and economically by Wartburg with a population of 150. In an attempt to thwart the pressure to move the county seat to Wartburg, the county court extended Montgomery's town limits to include both Wartburg and Sulphur Spring on the west side of the Emory River. This action, taken in August, was to no avail, and in October the sheriff was ordered to call a referendum and let the voters decide the location of the county seat. Each citizen was to write the name of his choice on the ticket–Montgomery, Wartburg, or Sulphur Spring.

Morgan County Courthouse, built 1870-71 in Wartburg. (Courtesy of Tennessee State Library and Archives, Nashville)

No record has been found of the result of this vote, but the fact that the courthouse remained at Montgomery speaks for itself.

In 1870 the question was raised again, and another referendum was authorized by the state. The citizens voted 195 to move the seat of government to Wartburg; 149 opposed. The county court recognized this vote as decisive and appointed a board of commissioners to dispose of county property in Montgomery and oversee building a new structure in Wartburg.

The county government advertised the sale of the Montgomery property in two newspapers, the Roane County *East Tennessean* and the *Press and Messenger,* and posted notices in three public places. Officials sold all the property except the county jail and the dressed stone around the jail and courthouse. Use of the courthouse was reserved by the county for 18 months.

The new courthouse in Wartburg was to be completed twelve months after the contract was let on June 6, 1870. The builders were A. J. Hurtt, Johann Kreis, and D. Kreis; they agreed to build the structure for $3132. Finished stone brought from the site of the old courthouse in Montgomery provided the foundation. The new courthouse was a frame structure containing four rooms for county offices, a jury room, and other rooms that the commissioners stipulated.

The county court did not wait for the new courthouse before it moved to Wartburg. On October 3, 1870, the court met at Montgomery; declaring that "the Court is not fully satisfied that said removal is fully recognized by all persons concerned and because there are those who recognize the sole power in the County Court to remove the County site absolute," the court resolved to move *that day* to Wartburg. The court directed the sheriff to procure a house to use until the new courthouse was finished. Then the justices journeyed to Wartburg and convened their second meeting on October 3 in the house of S. N. Staples. Lawyers followed the court and new courthouse to Wartburg, and by the end of the century six lawyers and two surveyors advertised their services in the *Morgan County Republican.*

Wartburg had two schools to serve its children. The oldest, operated by the Lutheran church, continued to educate German children. It had 80 students in 1870. A common school opened to accommodate other children. A third school called Wartburg Academy advertised for students in the *Republican* in 1895, offering instruction at 75¢ a month for primary students and at $1 to $1.50 a month for secondary and academy students. There is some doubt that this school ever opened because of opposition from the county court.

Wartburg had three churches in 1878, according to George Gerding. A Roman Catholic church served a small number of parishioners, a Presbyterian church absorbed several Swiss members of the disbanded Reformed congregation, and the Lutheran church continued as the principal house of worship. The Catholics had organized as early as 1847, then disbanded. In 1878 the group organized again and built a church the next year. Soon afterwards the building burned, supposedly destroyed by anti-Catholics. St. Paul's Lutheran Church became the center for the German population of the county. For some time after the

Civil War the church was without a pastor, and various laymen conducted the services. In the last three decades of the century the church secured pastors and conducted regular services. Until the beginning of the twentieth century these services were conducted in German; only after 1910 were English and German services given equal time.

Wartburg had a hotel and two saloons in the 1870s. Four general stores conducted business, operated by Francis Freytag, Rosa Kuhn, M. F. Redmon, and Hall and Brown. In the 1880s the Central Hotel was built and operated by M. F. Redmon; in the 1890s there were two other hotels, the Mountain, owned by J. H. Lewallen, and the Cumberland.

Railroad

Travel in and through Morgan County was still difficult and dangerous after the Civil War, and this lack of adequate transportation slowed economic recovery and prevented meaningful economic progress. Privately owned roads in the county were in poor condition, and the county had been completely neglected by railroad companies.

The Reverend A. B. Wright related some harrowing experiences on Morgan County roads which serve as good examples of their condition. One day in January of 1871 he became lost "in a dense wilderness" near Palestine Church, and a storm struck. Wind blew in the forest, and trees broke over his head. There was little light anywhere, and in his disorientation he traveled sixteen miles trying to cover eight. He finally found the house of Ervin Jones about seven at night, and, having missed his preaching appointment, stayed the night at Jones's house. Five years later, in the spring, he was again lost in Morgan County. This time he stayed the night with the Jack Hall family after stumbling on their house.

The nearest railroad to Morgan County was the Clinton to Knoxville line, about 30 miles east of Wartburg. Morgan County residents rode by horseback or in wagons to Winters Gap (later called Oliver Springs), which was one-half day's trip (17 miles)

Sunbright on July 4, 1888. (Courtesy of Charles Kreis)

from Wartburg. They stayed the night there before traveling the remaining 15 miles to Clinton to catch the train to Knoxville. Individuals or families might make this trip occasionally, but farmers and craftsmen found it unprofitable to take their products regularly to the Knoxville market this way.

The year 1880 opened the door to one of the most significant developments in the history of Morgan County. The Cincinnati Southern Railroad was completed from Chattanooga to Cincinnati, and it passed through Morgan County. Entering the county through Emory Gap and following the Emory River nearly to Lancing before climbing onto the plateau, the railroad passed south to north through the center of the county. Short lumber lines ran from the main line to Nemo and Pilot Mountain.

Sunbright, Lancing, and Oakdale were on the Cincinnati Southern route, and each profited and grew significantly as a result. Sunbright received its name with the coming of the railroad. It had earlier been called Stapleton; but the railroad station there was called Sunbright, and the town adopted that name, indicating the importance of the railroad to the town and county.

Lancing also received its name with the coming of the railroad. Called Kismet before, railroad employees called the station Lancing, and in 1894 the postal authorities accepted the new name. Founded in the 1860s, Lancing showed some growth with the building of the railroad. In 1879 Fordham's store opened, and later Buxton's Hotel operated in the building. Two churches, Methodist and Presbyterian, were organized in the 1880s. A town plat filed in 1880, consisting of 100 acres, laid off in blocks with named streets, anticipated a degree of growth for the town that never developed.

Oakdale profited most with the coming of the railroad. First called Honeycutt after the family who owned the land in the area along the Emory River, the name Oakdale was adopted in 1892 from the name of an abandoned settlement about ten miles southeast. The Cincinnati Southern wanted this particular land as a switching point for its trains headed north toward Somerset. The steep grade between Oakdale and Somerset demanded an extensive railroad yard for maintaining, refueling, and restructuring the trains. Water was readily available from the river, and coal from the surrounding area. The railroad bought a two-mile strip of land along the river from the Honeycutts, who had settled there about 1785, and operations which had been located at Glenmary and Rockwood were moved to the new yards at Oakdale.

In the nineteenth century all looked bright and prosperous for Oakdale. In 1892 the citizens built a new school, and the Babahatchie Inn was reconstructed, replacing one destroyed by fire the previous year. The original, built in 1880, and the replacement built in 1892 were identical. The buildings were two-story frame, used for housing both railroad employees and travelers. The first floor contained the dining room, lobby, and offices; the second had sleeping accommodations. Although the railroad built and owned the facility, it leased the management to individuals. In 1906 the Babahatchie became the railroad YMCA, one of the largest such operations in the world.

Oakdale was incorporated in 1887, then the only town in the county so dignified. Thirty-one of the 36 registered voters favored incorporation. In 1895 the General Assembly repealed the charter, but in 1911 the town was again incorporated.

In addition to the positive benefits accrued to these three specific towns, the entire county received its most significant economic opportunity with the coming of the railroad. Now the markets of the world were open to Morgan County products, which were still mostly raw materials. Lumber, livestock, and coal could be shipped to more profitable markets. Now the citizens of Morgan County could easily travel around the state, the nation, and the world; and the world could just as easily come to Morgan County, as did indeed happen in the second half of the nineteenth century.

Planned Settlements and Resorts

Morgan County was the scene of social experiments and business ventures because of its natural beauty, its ecology, and its available land. Despite contemporary evidence to the contrary, Morgan County was touted as an unusually healthy place to live or vacation, so a number of planned communities were established and advertised as health resorts or land ventures.

A Frankfort map described the area as "a natural all-the-year-round health resort. A climate free from the extremes of the temperatures of the north and the south. Frankfort is indeed a thing of beauty and joy forever. Frankfort has an abundant water supply." Frankfort's economic advantages were extolled with similar lack of modesty: "Frankfort is destined to become the manufacturing city of the Cumberland Plateau there can be no doubt; that it will also be a great distributing center of its section is equally true." The county surveyor, S. H. Staples, laid out the town with boulevards 80 feet wide, streets 66 feet wide, and alleys 14 feet wide. Residential lots were 50 x 132 feet and business lots 25 x 132 feet. Boulevards were named after presidents of the United States, and the streets were numbered one through seven. Some families from Wisconsin, Louisiana, Illinois, Maryland, and Iowa did take the bait and buy the land, but the development never lived up to the promises made by its promoters.

Deer Lodge was another land venture advertised as a health resort. In 1884 Abner Ross, manager of the Tabard Inn at Rugby, bought a tract of land at Deer Lodge that the Davidsons and Peter Fox had settled and owned. Ross promoted the settlement as an economic opportunity and a health resort. *The Southern Enterprise,* a newspaper published at Deer Lodge, carried the following advertisement in 1899:

> No healthier place on earth—the invalid's paradise. The climate is delightful, the elevation being about 1900 feet, making it an all-the-year-round health resort.
> Sufferers from catarrh, hay fever and kindred troubles receive immediate benefit, from a short sojourn in this lovely region. The water is safe, pure and is highly helpful for all kinds of kidney trouble.

In 1890 the Mountain View Hotel opened as a health resort. Owned and operated by Mrs. J. E. Struble, it was a square, two-story building with a veranda across the front on each level. A central staircase went through the roof to a covered platform on top of the building from which guests enjoyed a panoramic view of the beautiful countryside. Room rent was one dollar per day, with special rates for a week or a month. The Summit Park Hotel, just east of Deer Lodge, opened in the 1890s. Larger than the Mountain View, it was a three-story building with a dining room, kitchen, and two large rooms on the first floor, six bedrooms on the second floor, and four on the third.

Deer Lodge boasted a theater and a band to entertain its visitors, in addition to *The Southern Enterprise* (later *Deer Lodge Newsletter*) to inform them. Deer Lodge used the telephone line through Morgan County built in 1888 by the Genesis and Obed River Telephone Company. The line ran from Sunbright through Deer Lodge to Genesis, Crossville, and Sparta. In the winter of 1890 a heavy snow felled the lines, and housewives

The Ross Adkins Store at Deer Lodge, later converted into a medical clinic. (Courtesy of the *Morgan County News*)

exchanged their hickory bark withe or grapevine clotheslines for some of the telephone line. The phone company went bankrupt.

Some permanent settlers came to Deer Lodge from the North, mostly Polish miners and mill workers. A Dr. Ostrowski from Chicago may have been the first Polish settler about 1900. He attracted other settlers with his recommendation of the area as a healthy climate. S. T. Kimbell of Chicago opened a real estate agency in Deer Lodge and brought in many Poles from Pennsylvania. These settlers organized a Catholic church in the area, and one of their buildings was burned by the Ku Klux Klan in 1924.

A planing mill owned by the Whipple family was the most significant economic enterprise in Deer Lodge. It manufactured paneled doors, woodwork, and gingerbread decoration. When the Whipples left with their mill about the turn of the century, Deer Lodge declined as other residents departed. The community that *The Southern Enterprise* called "the leading settlement of the Plateau" in 1898 never recovered from this economic disaster.

Rugby was a socioeconomic experiment spawned by philosophical principle rather than by profit motive. It was the dream of English lawyer Thomas Hughes, advocate of the working class and author of *Tom Brown's School Days* and four other books. Hughes was educated at Rugby school in England, studying under Dr. Thomas Arnold, whose egalitarian philosophy and educational methods impressed him. Hughes was also influenced by Frederick Denison Maurice at Lincoln's Inn law school. Maurice, a Christian Socialist, promoted trade unions and education for the working class. Hughes became principal of Working Men's College in London after Maurice's death. As a member of Parliament from 1865 to 1874, he introduced a trades union bill to legalize labor unions. The bill did not pass.

With his general philosophy of egalitarianism and his emphasis on the nobility of labor, Hughes was concerned by the shiftless lives of members of the upper class in England. He was particularly concerned about younger sons, who were victims of the primogeniture system. Hughes knew that the United States had abolished primogeniture, and he liked the work ethic that prevailed in America. In 1870 he visited the United States for the first time; he was received as a well-known statesman and popular author by men of literature and government.

Hughes' visit culminated in his effort to establish a utopian agricultural colony in the United States for Englishmen. Morgan County became the location of his colony strictly by accident. The Panic of 1873 had created widespread unemployment in the northeastern industrial cities of the United States. In Massachusetts, the Boston Board of Aid to Land Ownership planned to send unemployed industrial workers to an agricultural colony in the South or the West. Franklin W. Smith, a Boston businessman, was to locate suitable land and purchase it. He took option on 350,000 acres in Morgan, Scott, and Fentress counties. Then economic conditions in the Northeast improved and the necessity and desire to move the workers disappeared. The land on the plateau was offered for sale.

At about this same time, 1879, Thomas Hughes created the Board of Aid to Land Ownership Limited, in England. He was president; John Boyle, Lord Montgomery, a London lawyer, was vice-president; and Henry Kimber, a British railroad magnate, was principal investor in the company. When Smith acquainted Hughes with the Tennessee land for sale, the Board of Aid bought 75,000 acres in 1880.

Activities culminating in the establishment of the colony moved quickly. Hughes returned to the United States in August of 1880 to oversee the creation of his dream. A hotel, the Tabard Inn, was immediately built to receive the first settlers and guests. A road seven miles long connected the new railroad to the new town. Opening day of the colony was set for October 5. All was done too quickly, without enough thought about the important economic necessities which would guarantee the success of the venture.

By October 5 Hughes expressed "serious misgivings" about opening the colony so soon. Only the upper floors of the hotel were complete. Construction materials still lay about. The walls of the church, where Hughes hoped to conduct his opening ceremonies, were only six feet above the ground. The road from the railroad track was finished, with trees and stumps removed, but the bridge was only partly completed, and approaches to it were "in a hopeless condition." To make the situation worse, "a great rain fell."

"After great difficulties" the guests were conveyed to the hotel and lodged. They enjoyed breakfast on opening day from six to nine. Then after some two hours of promenade in the gardens and on the lawn tennis grounds, the opening ceremony began on the veranda of the Tabard Inn at eleven. Visitors occupied chairs placed on the veranda and on the lawn. The service was a short one, with two psalms recited and a prayer offered by Bishop Charles Todd Quintard. After dinner visitors spent the afternoon admiring the natural beauty of the area; in the evening they gathered around a new piano in the hotel parlor for singing.

Thomas Hughes did not live in the colony, although a house

was built for him, and although his mother did become a permanent resident from 1881 to 1887. Hughes pursued his legal practice in England, becoming a county judge in 1882. He visited the colony annually, usually in August or September, until 1887.

The Board of Aid in London controlled the colony directly, which was a mistake and a great hindrance. A manager who represented the board lived in Rugby. Cyrus Clark, an American, held the position for the first few months, then vice president John Boyle took his place. In May of 1882 Robert Walton, a resident, assumed the post.

Another mistake concerned the terms of land sales to the settlers. Tracts of from 5 to 500 acres were offered, with one-fourth of the price required initially and the balance to be paid in three years at an interest rate of 6 percent.

About 200 settlers moved into Rugby in 1880, only about 80 of them English. Approximately 40 were from Tennessee, and about 80 from other states. By the beginning of 1884 the population had doubled, and this 400 was the high point of the colony's numbers. Although no exact figures are available, evidence indicates that most of the early residents were male. Hughes' niece Emmy continually complained in her letters about too many men and not enough ladies in the colony. Her grandmother Margaret Hughes invited only men to dinner because there were no ladies, and she mentioned a man playing the fairy in a drama because no ladies were available. Many of the single men were second sons of Englishmen, the group for whom Hughes had established the colony. They were called "remittance men" because they received financial aid from home. They usually had no skills to contribute to the success of the colony.

Some of the first residents lived in tents or log cabins; others lodged in the hotels until their homes were completed. Several of the "remittance men" lived alone in shanties.

Eventually the settlers constructed about 65 permanent buildings of all types. Brick and stone were not used, except in foundations, and most of the structures were of board-and-batten or clapboard construction. All of the finer homes displayed Victorian style decoration. Some were of English cottage design,

Tabard Inn. (Courtesy of Jimmy Keen, The Lindens, Rugby)

but John Boyle's house, Roslyn, was built in the more formal Georgian style. Twin Oaks, the home of Beriah Riddell, was a large two-story Victorian structure, nicknamed "the mansion" because of its size and its decoration. Its inside walls were plastered; most of the other homes used pine-paneled interiors.

The largest structure in the colony was the Tabard Inn, first built in 1880. This was a three-story structure with mansard roof and dormer windows. The first two floors were completely encircled with verandas. The inn was equipped with an excellent dining room, billiard tables, and courts for tennis and croquet. This structure burned in 1884 and was replaced with a larger and more elaborate second Tabard Inn in 1887. Built in the Eastlake style, this structure also had three floors. A multigabled roof, numerous chimneys, and several first-floor porches were all topped off by a lookout porch on the roof.

Newbury House was a large two-story structure with ten rooms and mansard roof, which was used as a guest house or hotel. Emmy Hughes thought that Newbury House was more

Christ Church, Episcopal (*on left*) and Thomas Hughes Free Public Library. (Courtesy of Tennessee State Library and Archives)

noted for cleanliness and for good food than the first Tabard Inn. After the second Tabard burned, the Newbury was the only hotel in town. A mail hack stopped at the door of Newbury House, delivering passengers and news to Rugby.

A large three-story rectangular school building, named in memory of Hughes' teacher Thomas Arnold, housed the educational institution of the colony as well as the church before its building was completed. This building had gothic style windows.

Christ Church and the Thomas Hughes Free Public Library were probably the most attractive buildings in the town. The church was built in carpenter gothic, which means wood construction rather than stone. It was paneled with pine and walnut and decorated with stained-glass windows. The vaulted roof supported by hand-hewn timbers gave the interior a cathedral look. Eight beautiful hanging lamps were brought from England, as was the rosewood organ.

The library, next door to the schoolhouse and across the street from the church, was the symbol of sophistication and culture in the settlement. A 40 x 30 foot clapboard building crowned by a clipped gable roof and cupola, the beautiful little building housed 7000 volumes of British and American literature donated by publishers honoring Thomas Hughes.

The colony was well equipped for leisure activities. In addition to the books in the library and the activities at the Tabard Inn, many other amusements beckoned. The Gentlemen's and the Ladies' Swimming Holes on the Clear Fork River provided refreshing entertainment on hot summer days, and the carefully designed trails were envigorating on crisp mornings and afternoons.

Numerous clubs and societies existed. A social club, billiard club, lawn tennis club, cricket club, and football club were formed. Masons, Odd Fellows Horticultural and Agricultural Society, and Rugby Public Purposes Association also provided information, service, and entertainment. Dances were held at the Tabard Inn, and a drama club performed about twice a month. Hughes' niece complained that the cornet band did not play "quite in tune," but she and other residents enjoyed their concerts. Five different newspapers were published in Rugby between 1881 and 1891, and a telephone line ran between the railroad and the Board of Aid in Rugby.

The English tea was a daily ritual. At the appointed hour labor ceased, workingmen bathed and donned their starched shirts to join the ladies for tea at the Tabard Inn. Then they might stroll on the lawns while waiting for dinner and a dance or concert at the Inn.

Emmy Hughes' description of a Christmas celebration in Rugby in 1885 might serve as illustration of the gala social scene in the settlement.

> We had rather a gay Xmas, with different sorts of Entertainments. On Xmas Eve there was a Xmas tree for the children at the Commissary Hall (where all Entertainments are held) & I had two cornet accompaniments to play, & take part in a tableau in the character of little red-ridinghood's grandmother! There were recitations & Band playing as well. The Rugby Cornet Band is quite an institution now & takes part in our public Entertainments. On the 26th the Social Club had a sort of special Xmas meeting, with singing & recitations & cornet playing &c. I had three accompts for various people to play then. On the evening of the 2nd of January the last & grandest of the Entertainments took place. The Musical & Dramatic Club performed a burlesque of Cinderella &

> Mrs. Lumley, Mr. Wilson & I played duets between the acts, & she or Mr. Wilson played the accompts to the songs in the play. I had also to play soft music when the fairy godmother made her. . . appearance. It all went off well, & after the performance there was a supper at the Newbury House for the members of the Club & some of their friends.

The colonists attempted some serious economic endeavor. Col. Joseph Killebrew of the Tennessee Bureau of Agriculture and Immigration told the Board of Aid that, although the soil was poor, certain crops could be produced. Killebrew recommended truck crops like cabbage, beans, and potatoes, and fruits like apples, grapes, pears, and strawberries. He also suggested tobacco. Grains, he said, would not grow well. Cattle and sheep could be raised for food and income. The colonists, however, did not follow this advice. Instead, they tried to raise, harvest, can, and market tomatoes. Organizing the Rugby Canning Co. in 1882, the corporation offered shares at $10 apiece. Hughes showed his support by purchasing some stock. A 100 x 20 foot structure built in 1883 housed the canning machinery, and about $2000 in equipment was ordered. A boiler, steam pipe, and other equipment were installed; labels for the cans, received from England, listed the tomato price in shillings rather than in cents. The cannery never operated because not enough tomatoes were raised to make the enterprise feasible; the canning equipment was finally converted for use as a steam laundry.

Rugby Pottery Company prepared a prospectus, but this enterprise was never organized. Clay in the area was suitable for such an endeavor, so this was a good opportunity lost.

Another cooperative enterprise, a general store, opened in 1880, offering stock certificates to the settlers at $5 a share. A 60 x 40 foot building housed the store, the post office, and an assembly hall. This business was profitable for some time, but as the colony failed, so did the store.

One source of income for the colony in its early years, when it was popular, was tourists. Rugby was a newsworthy item for publications all over the United States. Journalists were interested in this unique experiment of sending gentlemen to the wilderness and in Thomas Hughes' association with the experiment. *Harper's Weekly* featured Rugby in its October 16, 1880, issue, and other articles followed in other publications. Many times they tended to be skeptical of the colony's chances for success, but they were fascinated by the attempt. Many visitors came to see for themselves, drawn by curiosity or by Rugby's advertisements as a health resort.

Some of the claims were either false or would soon disappear. In 1881 Rugby's title to a healthy environment ended in a typhoid epidemic that killed seven young Englishmen. Twenty-one cases of typhoid developed, with the Tabard Inn well as the source of contamination. The inn closed, was repainted and refurnished, and Abner Ross of the Palmer House in Chicago was brought in to manage it. Travelers and visitors returned to the hotel in increasing numbers, but in 1884 it burned. Rebuilt in 1887, it burned again in 1899. The second Tabard had never realized a profit, so it was not rebuilt.

Emmy Hughes reported in 1886 that several houses in Rugby were empty. Margaret Hughes, Thomas' mother and Emmy's grandmother, died in 1887. After her burial Thomas never returned to the colony. All of these incidents were indications of, and causes for, the decline of the colony.

Despite the continued existence of the town of Rugby, Hughes' utopian agricultural colony failed. The reasons for its lack of success were numerous. The fact that Hughes himself never lived in the colony was one reason; the fact that his mother did live there and added some encouragement to the settlers was no substitute for his absence. Hughes would have been able to impress his ideas concerning labor and co-operative ventures on the community if his presence had been constant rather than sporadic, and his personal management of the colony might have been less disgruntling to the settlers.

The fact that the Board of Aid in London made the major decisions concerning Rugby helped contribute to the failure of the colony and to the dissatisfaction of the settlers with the management. Slow communications delayed implementation of decisions made in London and created problems for the settlers.

One family was obliged to live in a tent while waiting for the board to assign them a lot on which to build a house. With winter approaching, the wife became ill, and the delayed decision of the board became literally a matter of life and death.

The resident manager could not make specific but necessary decisions for the board, and the first two resident managers themselves became part of the problem. Cyrus Clark was unacceptable to the board, either because he was an American or because the board was attempting to economize. So the vice-president of the board, John Boyle, became second resident manager. He had no experience with such a position, and his personality was obviously unsuited to the job. The settlers were so disgusted and discouraged with his personality, attitude, and management methods that they nicknamed him "Lord John God Almighty Boyle."

Money does not appear to have been a problem for the settlers, but making money definitely was. The "remittance men" received allowances from their families in England, and they spent it freely. Instead of growing their own food or buying from other settlers, they ordered tinned foods from Cincinnati. Those who came to Rugby to make a living, however, had a difficult time. The terrain and the soil were not suited to the type of farming and products with which they were familiar. Even if they had been successful in producing crops on a commercial scale, transportation to the markets would have been too difficult and expensive. It was seven miles to the Cincinnati Southern track, which ran from Cincinnati to Chattanooga, but not to Knoxville, a nearer market. Cincinnati was already well supplied, while Chattanooga and Knoxville were not large enough for commercial markets. Wartburg, Huntsville, and Jamestown, the closest towns, had populations of only about 100 each, most of whom grew their own food.

The two most plentiful natural resources in the area, timber and coal, were not utilized by the Rugbeians. They did not have the skills to work the wood, nor did they have the transportation to move the coal.

Added to all these problems was lack of training, experience, and motivation among the settlers. Many of them did not have the rural and agricultural backgrounds needed for success in the wilderness. The experience of some of them, in the different soils, climates, and crops with which they were accustomed, was less useful in Morgan County. The motivation of others, notably the "remittance men," was not strong enough, in addition to the fact that they had no training or experience in manual labor. One must remember that it was not considered proper among this class to work with their hands. Hughes himself was unusual in believing that manual labor was noble, but even he did not put his philosophy into practice by dirtying his hands in Rugby. Hughes lost money in the Rugby experiment–about $250,000–but it was to large degree because of his own negligence.

In 1892 the Rugby Tennessee Company Limited was created with English money to take control of the holdings of the Board of Aid. In 1899 the Rugby Land Company, with American money, bought the land. By this time English Rugby had been absorbed into the rural America of Morgan County, as had German Wartburg been absorbed after the Civil War.

Brushy Mountain Prison

In addition to the building of Cincinnati Southern Railroad and the development of planned settlements and resorts, the construction and opening of Brushy Mountain Penitentiary was another important economic development in the last half of the nineteenth century. The building of the prison in Morgan County was not an accident, but developed out of the long history of Tennessee's prison problems, which have never been satisfactorily solved.

In January of 1893 both outgoing Governor John P. Buchanan and incoming Governor Peter Turney recommended to the General Assembly abolishing the convict lease system and building a second prison. In April the legislature responded, passing a bill calling for the construction of a penitentiary and purchase of both coal lands and farm land on which to work the inmates. Bonds totaling $600,000 financed these provisions.

Governor Turney appointed a committee of three men to select and puchase land for the prison, the farm, and the mines. They inspected the coal lands around Petros twice, conducting a thorough study. Dr. James M. Stafford, state geologist, observed, "There is no better coal property in the State of Tennessee."

The coal lands in Morgan County belonged to the East Tennessee Land Company. The firm owned about 12,000 acres, and the state wanted 9000. The contract, signed in August of 1893, stipulated that Tennessee was to pay $80,000 for the 9000 acres and that the East Tennessee Land Company was to build within six months twenty miles of railroad track from Harriman to the prison site. The Harriman Coal and Iron Railroad was already under construction along the designated route, so this task could be completed within the time schedule. In 1900 Tennessee purchased the Armes tract of 4226 acres and added it to the prison lands. This purchase enlarged the site for Brushy Mountain Penitentiary to about 13,000 acres. The boundary of Morgan County was extended into Anderson so that all this land would be in one county.

In July of 1894 the convict labor camp at Big Mountain closed, and the inmates moved to a camp near Harriman to construct the railroad track to Petros. Under the command of Captain G. H. Croser, the convicts worked with Cumberland Construction Company to lay the track. By the first of November the track was complete from Harriman to the State's coal tipple at Brushy Mountain; it was renamed Harriman and Northeastern Railroad. The 75 convicts who had been working on the track then replaced the free laborers who had developed the first coal mine at Brushy Mountain under the direction of L. E. Bryant, geologist and mining engineer. By January 1, 1896, the convicts were extracting a thousand tons a day.

The penitentiary, constructed north of Petros in a horseshoe shaped hollow at the foot of Frozen Head Mountain, was in a beautiful and secure position. Because it was almost completely surrounded by high mountains, escape would be difficult. The

First Brushy Mountain prison buildings and stockade, opened in 1896 (*below*) and the "manway" over which prisoners walked to the mines (*right*). (Courtesy of Charles Kreis)

building site was to the left and the rear of the later prison constructed in 1937.

The entire penitentiary was built of wood harvested from the dense forest that encompassed the site. Poplar, white oak, chestnut oak, cherry, walnut, and pine were in plentiful supply. Two sawmills turned the timber into lumber. Frank Schubert of Morgan County operated one of the mills, and a Mr. Bartley from Indiana the other.

The main building of the prison, an L-shaped structure designed by S. M. Patton of Chattanooga, was put up by free labor. A. W. Evans was construction engineer. The front of the structure was four stories high and formed a rectangle measuring 205 x 31 feet. The wing which formed the L on the west was three stories, 170 x 31 feet. All the walls consisted of rough-finished, one-inch thick planks set perpendicular, and spaces between the planks were covered with strips in a board-and-batten style. The inside walls were of dressed pine, laid diagonally. Floors also consisted of double construction with tarpaper between. The lower

oner loaded several tons of coal each day, the exact amount depending on the thickness of the seam. In this way he repaid his debt to the state. Inmates might even earn money—from 5¢ to 40¢ a ton—by working "overtask." Those who did not work the mines drove teams, performed repair and maintenance work, made coke, worked at the tipple, cooked, or labored in the laundry or hospital. Trusties worked in prison offices or in prison officials' homes. The sixty-acre farm also provided employment for prisoners. Until 1903 twelve hours was a normal work day.

In 1916 the state used 225 prisoners in Campbell County to build the Jellico highway through a difficult section of the mountains. In 1919, 125 convicts worked in a lumber camp at Fork Mountain to harvest timber that belonged to the state. Tennessee realized almost $500,000 from this operation.

Punishment for inmates guilty of offenses within the prison consisted of confinement in the dungeon, a cell six feet by three feet with no furniture. Whipping with a wide leather strap was another punishment, and the most severe was "suspension," hanging the offender by his thumbs from a hook in the ceiling so that his toes just touched the floor. This punishment lasted from five to thirty minutes.

If prisoners escaped from Brushy Mountain a steam whistle sounded once for each escapee, and blood hounds and mounted guards pursued. The men of Petros joined the hunt because of a $25 standing reward for any escaped prisoner returned and because of concern of their own safety.

The development of Petros and Coalfield related to the establishment of Brushy Mountain Penitentiary. Many of the residents of Petros worked at the prison or on the Harriman and Northeastern Railroad. The town was not a marketplace of any significance, and its only commercial establishments were service businesses. The first name for the village was Joynersville, but the post office changed the name to Petros in 1895. "Richburg" was another name for the area about 1895, for some deeds refer to this name, and a town plat for Richburg identical with that of Petros was filed with the county court in 1895. However, the name "Petros" prevailed. "Petros" has been interpreted as "the rock,"and is said to refer either to the mountain or to the prison.

Coalfield, a town older than Petros and the prison, was a community of farmers, carpenters, and millwrights before the prison was built. The Harriman and Northeastern Railroad already ran as far as Coalfield, or "Ruffner's Station"as it was called at the time, before the state ordered it to be extended to the site of the new prison. The railway provided transportation to markets for the area's coal, and coal mining occasioned the town's new name of Coalfield in 1900. Several mines opened, and between 1900 and 1915 the town's population doubled.

Life in Morgan County, 1865–1900

The population of the country grew significantly between the end of the war and the beginning of the new century. After dropping during the Civil War decade to 2969, the population grew very quickly to 5156 in 1880 and to 9587 in 1900. This 300 percent increase indicates the tremendous economic influence that the building of the Cincinnati Southern Railroad, the development of planned settlements and resorts, and the establishment of Brushy Mountain with its railroad had upon the county. Morgan County recovered quickly from the Civil War largely because these catalyts provided new economic life for the county.

Most residents of the county engaged in agriculture after the war, and most farmers still operated on the subsistence level. Joseph Killebrew, Tennessee Bureau of Agriculture, reported in 1870 that rotation was little used in the county. "Corn follows corn, year after year." Some, he observed, did alternate oats and wheat with corn. The bull-tongued plow was normally used, which plowed too shallow and created foul fields. Killebrew suggested deep plowing and thorough cleaning of the land.

In 1870 there were 394 farms in Morgan County, most of them only 20 to 50 acres, and only eight were between 100 and 500 acres. In 1880, with the significant increase in population, the number of farms doubled to 619, and by 1890 there were

906, averaging 137 acres in size. Wright thought that the land in the area would produce five to six barrels of corn and 100 bushels of Irish potatoes per acre. Improved farm land sold in 1870 for $5 to $20 per acre at six percent interest. By 1882 the average value of the improved land was $1.52 per acre. Roane County land was valued at $8.32, and Scott at $1.16.

In the last half of the nineteenth century corn was the most popular crop in Morgan County, with almost 110,000 bushels produced in 1860 and 130,000 in 1900. Production of some other crops, such as wheat and tobacco, actually decreased. Sweet potato and Irish potato production increased between 1860 and 1900, but not in significance to the increased number of farms. Production tended to go down during the decade of the Civil War, and in the cases mentioned above it did not reach pre–Civil War levels by the end of the century.

Specialty plants were grown to some extent. Killebrew complained that few fruits were grown in1870, although the county's soil and climate were well-suited for apples and peaches. He did compliment the Germans around Wartburg for growing grapes and producing wine, which brought the high price of $4 per gallon. Sorghum and maple sugar were made and used in Morgan County, and "the finest honey in the world is produced here." By 1880 the value of orchard products grown in the county was $8190. According to the 1890 report, 46,915 bushels of apples and 5485 bushels of peaches were picked. In 1900 farmers harvested 106 bushels of cherries. The value of orchard products in 1890 was $27,110. Killebrew would have been pleased. Three 500-pound bales of cotton were grown on eleven acres in 1900, but the soil and climate were not suited for this crop.

Joseph Killebrew noticed little improvement in the county's livestock in 1870. He observed no improved breeds of horses, cattle, hogs, or sheep; the animals were of "scrub species." He found few mules in the county, but said that oxen were used for work on the rough terrain. Peter Fox started a sheep ranch near Deer Lodge in 1876, but he soon lost 150 of his stock to wild

One of the first houses in Petros, built about 1855, with square notched logs, a stone chimney, loft room, and a shed addition at the rear. (Courtesy of Charles Kreis)

animals. Fox was so discouraged that he sold out to Abner Ross in 1884.

Killebrew thought that Morgan County farmers should pursue livestock production; he was particularly impressed with the natural possibilities for the dairy business. He noted, however, "everything is blank on this subject." Some grasses grew well in the climate and soil, but farmers had not improved their pastures. Instead, they tended to burn off the stubble, hoping to make the grass grow early each year. Killebrew thought this practice added a few days growth, but it also destroyed humus and timber.

Overall production of livestock did improve during the last half of the nineteenth century. Between 1860 and 1890 mules, horses, oxen, cows, and sheep all increased, though not significantly.

Two of the large landowners and farmers in the county after

the Civil War were Victor Letorey and John Boyle, Lord Montgomery. Boyle, vice-president to the Board of Aid in the Rugby settlement, owned about 3500 acres. After his sojourn in Rugby, he returned to live in London; but for some time he made annual visits from England to his farm, bringing large parties of guests with him to hunt. Letorey, born in New Orleans of French parents, moved to Morgan County after the Civil War because of the area's climate and scenery. He bought 800 acres of forested land just east of Wartburg. Although he had had no experience in agriculture, he was trained in chemistry. On his Morgan County land he experimented with grapes and wine making and with the breeding of cattle.

Another large landowner in the county was Christian Melhorn, who had 1356 acres of land southwest of Wartburg on the Emory River. He came to the German colony in 1847 and lived on his land until after the war. The town of Deermont, originally called the Melhorn settlement, was established in conjunction with his farm.

Industry increased in Morgan County after the Civil War. This is not to deny, however, that agriculture was still the predominant occupation and economic force. In 1860 there were only eight manufacturing operations employing 20 men in the county, and this included two coal mines. Other operations in 1860 were two gristmills, three sawmills, and one tanyard. The total value of the manufactured products, including coal, was $27,000. In 1870 the first steam engine appeared in the manufacturing report, but the number of manufacturing establishments had fallen to seven and the value of manufactured products to $13,676. The war had done its damage. In 1880 the figures had declined more, but by 1900 the industrial figures had increased dramatically. The number of establishments was up to 38 and the number of workers to 87. Value of the manufactured products was $146,937.

Much of this increase in product value was in coal production. The Cincinnati Southern and the Harriman and Northeastern railroads created the opportunity for coal markets outside the county. In the early 1880s several mines opened on

Indian Creek, and mines opened on the short railway to Catoosa. When the Harriman and Northeastern was finished mines opened along it at Petros, Stephens, and Coalfield, and a mine operation opened on the Cincinnati Southern land at Oakdale in 1896. Thus, the county improved its economy significantly with the coming of railroads and development of the mines.

After the Civil War rural life did not change quickly. Both Killebrew and Wright reported in the 1870s that most of the homes were log, but Wright insisted that they were "very comfortable in the winter." Large fireplaces provided heat, and most housewives also cooked in them. The "cook-stove" was a rare appliance. Fireplaces made with stick and clay chimneys increased fire hazards. Killebrew reported a few brick houses and a number of frame dwellings in the 1870s, when lumber cost approximately one dollar per hundred foot. Fences were also made of wood—rail "worm fences" about five feet high. The fence corners grew briers and bushes, and the fences rotted rapidly. Rails cost about ten dollars per thousand.

Farm families occupied their days almost entirely in producing food. Most of the families did the work themselves, and Killebrew observed that "all are trained to industrious habits." Wright agreed that the whole family would work in the field all day. In addition most had cows and work animals to tend. In the home women made clothes and preserved food. Some still manufactured cloth on the spinning wheel and loom, using wool or the small amount of cotton that could be grown. Cowhides were tanned with a solution of oak bark acid, and homemade shoes were held together with wooden pegs. Shoe strings might be fox, squirrel, or groundhog hide.

Preserving food for use over the winter was a major operation, since glass jars were not in general use in the area until near the end of the century. Meats were dried or smoked. Fruits, peas, and beans were also dried. Cabbage was made into kraut or buried in a hole and covered with straw and dirt. Beans, corn, cucumbers, beets, and other vegetables could be pickled. Corn was also dried in a crib, after which it was either taken to the gristmill to be ground into meal for bread, or it was made into hominy

The Kamer family and their log home beyond Potter Falls near Wartburg in the early twentieth century. (Courtesy of Charles Kreis)

by soaking it in lye to remove the husks, washing it thoroughly, and boiling it until tender.

In addition to working in the fields and caring for the animals, men provided additional food by hunting. Game was plentiful in Morgan County—wild hogs, deer, turkey, squirrels, and opossum. A farmer used his rifle or fish trap for catching fish because there were no fish hooks.

There was not a great deal of time for leisure activities in a life of subsistence farming, but A. B. Wright said many residents were "great readers;" he sold them thousands of books, mostly on religious subjects. In 1871 he sold Morgan Countians $40 worth of Methodist books and $200 worth of books from Goodspeed Publishing Company. Before 1900 the county had a number of newspapers, indicating a sufficient reading public. Before 1876 there was evidently no newspaper; Morgan County deed notices appeared in a Roane County paper. Several papers, beginning with the *Rugbeian* in 1881, were published in that settlement. Three papers were published in Wartburg during the last quarter of the nineteenth century. J. W. Kennedy was the proprietor of the *Morgan Dispatch* in 1876. In 1881 Landon H. Baker published the *Cumberland Plateau*. R. D. (Bud) Delius published the *Morgan County Republican* in the last half of the 1890s.

One of the most significant occurrences in the South after the Civil War was the development of public education, with the counties and the states assuming the obligation of educating children. Morgan County played its part in this drama.

The first superintendent of public education in the county may have been Lewis F. Nitzsche, whose bonding was recorded in the County Court Minute Book, January 4, 1869. In August of that same year the new superintendent, Charles H. Delius, reported that the county had schools in all civil districts, and in each subdistrict except one. In 1873 the Wartburg Public Schools received $450 in aid from the Peabody Fund, but in 1876 the superintendent, E. H. Booth, reported no public schools operating in the county because of indebtedness; in 1877 school was held in only one district. By 1878 there were 28 schools in session, thanks to additional property and poll tax money as well as state contributions and local subscriptions. School tax at this time was 10¢ on $100 of property evaluation. School sessions were generally three months in length, and there were between 20 and 50 schools operating in any given year between 1870 and 1899, with the exception of the years noted above. School buildings were usually log construction until 1885, when frame structures predominated. By 1899 most of the buildings were frame, with only five log structures remaining.

S. H. Jestes of Wartburg decribed classes in a log building: "School . . . was taught in a log school house with benches made of slabs of wood, . . . and the only thing that induced students to sit erect was the warp of black gum switch, as the benches had no backs. The course of study included Webster's speller, Smith's grammar, Davies & Ray's arithmetic, dictionary, geography, etc."

In 1870 the state constitution required segregated schools.

Sunbright Seminary was built about 1890. (Courtesy of Charles Kreis)

Morgan County, with a relatively small black population (30 to 50 children of school age) had no public education for them between 1876 and 1893, when the superintendent reported one school open for "colored." The report of the state superintendent showed no blacks in Morgan County schools until 1895, when 30 attended.

Morgan County had at least two academies after the Civil War to provide education beyond the grammar school level. The oldest, Walden Academy, had been operating at least since the 1830s. It was chartered a second time in 1877. Mt. Vernon Academy opened in 1891 in Burrville. The Methodist church operated it, and in 1900 changed its name to Wright Memorial Institute to honor the longtime circuit rider of the area, A. B. Wright. The school enrolled 60 students during its first year. The Methodists also operated Sunbright Seminary about 1890 in a two-story building east of the railroad. Each floor contained one room heated by a coal stove, with the stairway ascending the outside of the building.

Education and religion were close allies in the rural South

during the nineteenth century in that the churches sponsored a large percentage of the schools until public systems were established. Sunday Schools had an educational purpose, and church buildings were used as schools during the week. Preachers often acted as teachers. Circuit riders like A. B. Wright were book salesmen, spreading knowledge as well as religion.

Churches were social centers for rural populations. Quarterly meetings, class meetings, basket meetings or suppers, and love feasts in Morgan County were social gatherings as well as religious ceremonies. "Protracted meetings" continued for days or even weeks at "campgrounds" and drew large crowds seeking social and religious experiences. One such campground existed near the second Montgomery. People brought food and stayed at least all day. Some camped at night. Singing and preaching continued all the time.

Morgan County was predominantly Protestant, as was the state and the South; however, Morgan County could boast some unusual denominations. St. Paul's Lutheran Church in Wartburg and the two Lutheran churches at the Melhorn and Ruppe settlements south of Wartburg were uncommon congregations in the South. The Swiss Reformed Church in Wartburg was even more unusual. The Congregational Church, rare in the South, was established at Deer Lodge, and the Christ Church Episcopal at Rugby would have been more common on the east coast. Catholic churches in Wartburg and Deer Lodge represent the European and northern American immigration into the county. Indeed, all these churches represent the peoples of other countries and states bringing their beliefs with them when they moved to Morgan County, thus creating an ecumenical atmosphere.

The usual southern Protestant churches—Baptist, Methodist, and Presbyterian—cooperated to an extent that might have seemed unusual at another time and place. The Reverend Wright, a Methodist, reported holding communion with the Baptists, preaching in the home of a Baptist (Thomas Taylor), and using the Baptist building in Sunbright for Methodist services.

Wright's experience illustrates how difficult a minister's life was in the nineteenth century, how dangerous life in Morgan County might be, and how unorganized and occasional the practice of religion was. Wright was a circuit rider, and this was one of the most difficult religious "callings." He worked the Wartburg circuit in the 1870s, which included all of Morgan County, three appointments in Scott County, and one in Fentress. One year he traveled 1918 miles on horseback, preached 152 times, secured 63 subscribers to the Methodist *Advocate*, sold $40 in books, baptized 40 adults and 18 infants, and married one couple. His salary was $215, and he had to farm in addition to preaching to make a living. He lost his way a couple of times on Morgan County roads, as recounted earlier. On another occasion he was almost killed; riding to a quarterly meeting in March of 1875, he had to cross the Clear Fork River, swollen by rain. His horse was swept into the rapid waters and almost drowned; Wright was saved by a young man named Thomas Brewster in a canoe.

One of the major concerns of Protestant churches after the Civil War was alcoholic beverages, and Wright was active in the prohibition movement. Wartburg had two saloons in the 1870s, the Chattanooga Bar Room and the John D. Kreis saloon, both on Main Street. The Hole-in-the-Wall was Oakdale's tavern, and Wright mentioned two saloon-keepers in Kismet (Lancing), which he thought to be "the most wicked place" on his circuit. Rugby forbade consumption of alcohol within its limits, except for wine, and the Rugby Total Abstinence Society inforced the prohibition.

Wright was Morgan County chairman of the Tennessee Prohibition Committee. In 1887 he supported a proposed amendment to the state constitution prohibiting the sale of intoxicating liquors and spoke for two weeks in the county before the referendum. On August 25 he was to speak in Sunbright at the Baptist church; but the Reverend Summers, the Baptist minister, locked the doors, and Wright had to hold his rally in a nearby building. On September 8 he spoke at Wartburg. Everywhere he found the majority of Morgan County voters favored the sale of liquor, and on voting day the citizens rejected the amendment although most of East Tennessee was in favor of it.

The nineteenth century ended with the popular Spanish-American War of 1898. Incensed by newspapers against the Spanish repression of rebellion in Cuba, Americans were anxious to protect their women and their flag and to help the Cuban underdogs. The young men of 1898 did not remember the horrors of the American Civil War and they were anxious to express their manhood. The nation needed no draft system for this popular war, for which notables like Assistant Secretary of the Navy Theodore Roosevelt volunteered.

Capt. John W. Staples, a Wartburg native who practiced law in Harriman after 1890, was a popular recruiter for soldiers in Morgan County. After war was declared on April 28, Staples recruited about 75 Morgan County men for the Fourth Tennessee Regiment. Others traveled to Nashville to join the First Tennessee Regiment there. Altogether about 200 from Morgan County volunteered for service, which was many more than her quota. The First Regiment trained in San Francisco and fought heroically at Manila in the Philippines. The battle was so ferocious that Colonel Smith, the regiment commander, died of heat prostration. The Fourth Regiment was sent to Cuba, but it saw little action. When the four Tennessee regiments returned late in 1899, they were welcomed by the new governor, Benton McMillin.

The New Century

The international character of Morgan County's population was still apparent at the beginning of the century. The 1920 census showed 149 foreign-born residents in the county. Most came from Germany and Austria, but 20 others were born in Poland, 12 in England, and 12 in Canada. A number of Poles moved into the county around 1920, settling in the area of Deer Lodge, but most of them came from other parts of the United States. Only six of the ninety-five counties in Tennessee had more foreign-born residents than Morgan County, in spite of her small total population.

The population increase was not as heavy in the first three decades of the twentieth century as it had been in the last three decades of the nineteenth century. The increase of over 19 percent in the first decade began to fall, to 16 percent in the second decade, and 2½ percent in the third. This trend led to an actual decline in population after World War II.

Towns in the county grew during the first decades of the new century. The most populous was Oakdale, with a population of 1552 in 1920. The Cincinnati Southern railroad, choosing Oakdale as a major switching point, was the cause of its growth. The railroad's monthly payroll in Oakdale in 1914 was about $42,000. Oakdale Bank and Trust was organized in 1911 and Depositors State Bank in 1930 to handle the money and finance the growth of the town. The YMCA shared its clientele with four other hotels and a number of rooming houses. Private homes were going up by the dozen. Five general stores, one drugstore, one hardware store, several grocery stores and meat markets, one bottling works, and a furniture store supplied the physical needs of the growing population by 1914; three schools, two churches, six secret orders, and one newspaper supplied their intellectual and moral needs. Four doctors, one dentist, and two lawyers practiced in the town.

Petros was the second largest town in the county during the first part of the century, with a population of 1013 in 1930. The prison, coalmining, and the railroad provided for the fast growth of this town. Petros had a high school until 1926, when it was discontinued and the students transferred to the Wartburg school.

The county seat, Wartburg, experienced some physical and some professional growth in the early twentieth century, although its population was only about 500 in 1920. In 1904 the county built a new brick courthouse, with the brick laid in Flemish bond and the structure reflecting some of the characteristics of H. H. Richardson's Romanesque style. Cost to the county was $18,000. The Citizens Bank opened in 1906 and constructed its two-story brick building with two columns in 1923. The new brick school was dedicated in May of 1924. *Morgan County Press* began publication in

1909 view of Wartburg from Lutheran Church. (Courtesy of Charles Kreis)

Wartburg in 1916, and the *Morgan County News* succeeded it in 1926. The Hotel Zumstein, the Cumberland Hotel, and the Williams House welcomed guests to Wartburg. Four general stores, one clothing store, one hardware store, and a billiard parlor catered to the needs of customers in the 1920s. There were also four fraternal orders and two lodge halls. Wartburg boasted about seven lawyers and two doctors in this period.

Sunbright received some economic activity from the railroad, but oil and gas were the exciting features of the town's economy in the early twentieth century. Four companies specializing in the production of crude oil and natural gas and in refining gasoline and its byproducts located in Sunbright. Lumbering and coal mining were other profitable economic activities. Sunbright had two hotels and two general stores in 1920. By 1939 it had a bank, a high school, and an estimated population of 450. Dr. S. H. Jones was the physician in Sunbright.

Coalfield, with a population of 310 in 1930, profited from the Harriman and Northeastern Railroad. The town developed the natural resources of coal, timber, truck farming, and stock raising to take advantage of the markets the railroad opened; it developed its own business in the form of two lumber- and gristmills by 1920. Five stores, four churches, and two schools served the population.

Lancing, with no industry by the 1930s, was a depot and loading

Morgan County Courthouse, built in 1904, as it appeared in 1908. (Courtesy of Charles Kreis)

point on the Cincinnati Southern Railroad. It's population of 250 in 1930 was supported by the timber industry and agriculture. Three churches and a grade school were focal points in the community.

Deer Lodge, though it declined after the Whipple mill closed, still had a weekly newspaper, *Southern Enterprise*. It had three churches, including a Catholic and a Congregational. The town absorbed an influx of Polish settlers, and supported two medical doctors, T. W. Nash and Milton De Colbert. De Colbert held the Ph.D. as well as the M.D. and claimed to speak French, German, Russian, Polish, and Italian. The population of Deer Lodge in 1930 was 155.

Agriculture and Industry

The size of farms in Morgan County decreased in the first thirty years of the twentieth century, from an average size of 110 acres in 1900 to 84 acres in 1930; but this was true of the state as a whole. The average Morgan County farm remained about ten acres larger than the average Tennessee farm for the whole period. In 1930 Morgan County was 78th in the state in the number of farms.

With the railroads and the better highways of the twentieth century Morgan County agricultural products could be transported to the large markets. Farmers moved away from the subsistence farming system of the nineteenth century and specialized in cash crops. Fruits—apples, peaches, cherries, grapes, and strawberries—were well-suited for Morgan County's soil and climate and they became specialty crops. The *Morgan County Press* reported three fruit orchards "on an extensive scale" near Deer Lodge and Sunbright in 1916. In 1923 John A. Jones, William McIntyre, and A. S. Shadow opened the Cumberland Plateau Nurseries to produce fruit trees for transplanting. Strawberry farmers formed the Cumberland Plateau Fruitgrowers Association in the same year. Its members reported that 200 acres of strawberries in the county averaged a profit of $100 an acre.

Potatoes were another special cash crop that Morgan County farmers wisely chose in the early twentieth century. In 1923 the first railroad car of Irish potatoes, containing 600 bushels, was shipped to Birmingham, Alabama. They sold for $1.40 per bushel. The *Press* claimed that the Irish potato had become the "leading source of income" on small farms in the county. In 1924, 800 acres of potatoes were planted, but because of low prices that year, only 500 acres were planted in 1925.

Although livestock production was still part of the agricultural economy, it was not a specialty for Morgan county. Swine, goat, and sheep production all declined from 1900 to 1930. The county dropped from 14th to 22nd in state rankings for sheep-wool production, and this decline caused great concern. Several "sheep meetings" were held in the county in 1923 to promote this enterprise, and the Morgan County Sheep Growers organization campaigned for "sheep on every farm." The decline continued, however. The number of cattle produced remained stable, and there was a change to quality breeds and to beef stock.

Mechanization entered the Morgan County agricultural

scene with internal combustion vehicles and implements. In 1923 Citizens Motor Company of Wartburg became the dealer for Fordson tractors and attachments. By 1930 there was over $157,000 worth of farm machinery in the county. In the 1940s there were 179 tractors and two hay balers.

Scientific farming, increased production, and higher prices were the goals of organizations, such as the Cumberland Plateau Fruitgrowers Association, the Truck Growers Association, the Morgan County Potato Growers Association, and Morgan County Sheep Growers, all founded in the 1920s. The county court formed an agricultural committee to promote farming. Schools had agricultural clubs—corn, potato, and tomato clubs—to emphasize scientific farming. In 1915 the county court offered $300 as awards for the greatest production in these clubs.

Particularly significant in promoting these goals was the appointment of an agricultural agent for the county. J. A. Kyker was Emergency Demonstration Agent in 1917 and 1918, when increased production was emphasized as part of the war effort. R. L. Lyons was county agent from 1922 to 1926. C. R. Barnes was agent in the early 1930s, and E. L. Perry served from 1936 to 1940. The agent's duties included visiting farms, circulating informational letters to farmers, preparing educational columns for the newspaper, and organizing educational meetings and clubs. In 1926 the county court abolished the agent's position as an economy measure; Lyons had been paid $1200 annually. In 1931 the position was refunded, and in 1936 Morgan County associated with the Tennessee Farm Bureau. Forty-one farmers joined the organization within a week.

Before 1900 Morgan County had no banks, but in the first 30 years of the twentieth century five banks were chartered. The first was in Petros in 1904, the Morgan Bank and Trust Company. Others were founded in 1906, 1911, 1926, and 1930 in Wartburg, Oakdale, and Sunbright. The last was Depositors State Bank in Oakdale. The establishment of these financial institutions indicated increased economic activity and provided funds to generate additional enterprise. It is also significant that three of these banks eventually closed their doors.

In the twentieth century the county wanted to diversify its economy and attract manufacturing industry. In 1929 the county court published a resolution to "extend . . . a cordial invitation to industry." The court promised ten years exemption from county property tax on the site and the building. No manufacturing industry accepted, however.

The extraction and shipment of Morgan County's vast and valuable raw materials did increase. Coal, timber, and oil production accelerated significantly. The nation's demand for coal increased steadily after 1900, and the price increased in 1915 and 1916 before stabilizing in 1917. In 1923 production of coal reached a high point; then the market declined somewhat. Mines in the United States increased in number by more than 33 percent between 1909 and 1919. Morgan County was fourth in production of coal in Tennessee in 1910.

In Morgan County most of the coal mining was in the vicinity of Petros, Coalfield, and Oliver Springs. By 1910 convict workers were producing about 350,000 tons a year. There were some small mines between Coalfield and Christmas Siding on the railroad, and the Big Mountain Mine operated near Oliver Springs. Near Oakdale, Catoosa, and Nemo there were several other mines. Oakdale Coal Company opened about 1925, and the Taylor Coal Company operated near Nemo. In 1925 there were 37 companies with mining operations in Morgan County. In 1917 a dynamite blast ignited a dust explosion in the mines at Catoosa, killing 11 miners.

Logging was one of the first economic activities in Morgan County, and the lumber industry came with the first sawmills; but about 1900 timber became big business. A group of investors in Nashville controlled about 50,000 acres of forest in Morgan, Fentress, and Cumberland counties. In 1910 the Tennessee Mineral & Lumber Company initiated operations around Catoosa. Hundreds of workers were employed in the logging, sawmill, and railroad operations. Catoosa became a town of many buildings, among them a company store with monthly business of

Miners leaving a coal mine in Petros in the 1920s. Note oil lamps on caps and the mule used to pull coal car from the mine. (Courtesy of Charles Kreis)

$15,000. A destructive flood in 1929 and the depression of the thirties destroyed the lumber business and the town.

In 1917 the state decided to sell some timber on its prison lands in Morgan County; much of it had been stolen or lost to natural causes. The New River Camp was built at Fork Mountain, five miles from the prison, to be used as a lumber operation. Some of the trusty prisoners, totaling 125, were selected to cut and mill the timber. In 1918 about $330,000 worth of timber was sold, and the next two years an additional $150,000 was realized.

By 1926, 23,453,000 board feet of lumber had been cut and milled in Morgan County, wholesaling for a value of $630,367. A valuable industry for employment, 387 men worked in timber that year.

The newest business exploiting the natural resources of Morgan county was oil and gas. The first explorations in the county occurred in the Sunbright area about 1916. By 1917 there was one gas well at Sunbright, five oil and one gas well in the Rugby Road district, and two wells drilled in the Wartburg district. In

Band mill at Catoosa, c. 1915-1917. (Courtesy of Michael R. O'Neal)

1924 another flurry of drilling occurred in the Sunbright and Burrville area. Both oil and gas were produced, with the Bone Camp field northwest of Sunbright proving the most productive. By 1927 there were about 15 wells in the Sunbright area. Crude oil was piped to Sunbright for loading into tank cars, and Sunbright homes used natural gas. The Russell Producing Company of Sunbright owned the only completely equipped refinery in Tennessee in 1939. It produced and distributed Tenn Pep products.

Railroads in Morgan County provided a major means of transporting agricultural and industrial products out of the county in the early twentieth century. In addition to the Cincinnati Southern (now the CNC & TP), short lines projected into the county to carry products out. The Southern Railway and the Louisville and Nashville entered the county at Oliver Springs to pick up coal. The Harriman and Northeastern came through De Armond Gap for the same purpose in Coalfield and Petros. The Morgan & Fentress line ran from Nemo along Indian Creek and Turkey Creek to Obed Junction. M&F was 21 miles long, with all but one of those miles in Morgan County. Emory River Lum-

Locomotive No. 2 of the Morgan and Fentress Railway. Men on the cab are Roy Brown and Levi Kreis. (Courtesy of Michael R. O'Neal)

ber Company railroad ran from Lancing to the Emory River. From there one branch went up the Emory River and Greasy Creek; another ran through Wartburg and up Flat Creek.

Highways were a continual problem for the county because of the heavy expenses involved. A poor road system hindered economic development as long as road costs were locally financed. Only with the influx of state and federal monies did road improvements make travel easy in the county.

In the nineteenth century many roads in the county had been privately owned turnpikes. In the early twentieth century the county built and maintained all public roads. Large amounts of money were expended to construct and improve highways. In 1915 a $270,000 bond issue was voted to "macadamize" the county roads, but the next year voters defeated a second bond issue. In 1917 the legislature authorized a $200,000 bond issue without a county referendum. Forty miles of road were completed and 40 more miles were graded. Cost of that year's construction was $270,000, and the work was incomplete. In the early 1920s Morgan reached out to neighboring counties, macadamizing roads to Fentress and Scott counties.

Private entrepreneurs maintained roads. Contracts were let on bid, and each contractor maintained only a few roads or miles of roads. The superintendent of the road commission supervised the work. Residents were bound by law to two days of road work or $2.50 payment for maintenance of roads, but this law was largely ignored. In 1921 Morgan County was allowed to increase the tax to $7.50 or 27 hours work. All of this expense was burdensome to county budgets. In 1923 all county funds were depleted and the road fund was overdrawn by $100,000.

Residents of the county were not happy with the condition of their roads. The editor of the *Press* complained in 1920 that the road from Deer Lodge to Sunbright was "rapidly disintegrating under lumber trucks & wagons." One merchant from Petros commented, "If the public knew my real thoughts (about roads) I might be arrested." A miner retorted, "I can't think of words to express my feelings."

Relief appeared in the 1920s in the form of state and federal aid. Governor Austin Peay started a state road program in 1923, financed by a 2¢ gas tax. Between 1923 and 1930 the mileage of surfaced roads tripled in the state. In 1922 a new state and federal highway through Morgan County was announced. Named Dixie Air Line Highway (US 27), it was completed in 1926 and connected Morgan County to Cincinnati and Chattanooga. It provided the major artery for the county. In 1926 the state highway department also agreed to maintain the main roads in the county. Thus an enormous financial burden was lifted from the county budget.

Life in Morgan County, 1900–1930

By the beginning of the Great Depression, life in the county had improved significantly from the nineteenth century. Clapboard and brick homes replaced log structures, and the modern homes were equipped with appliances developed by modern technology. The Central Telephone Company, operating in the county in the first decade of the new century, installed 52 phones in Wartburg and 150 in Oakdale by 1916, the only two areas to have phone service at this time. Charge for a phone was $1.50 per month. By 1930 there were 213 phones in the county.

The first electric power in the county was installed at Brushy Mountain Prison. About 1910 Hamilton Woods of Petros electrified his mine and 40 mine shacks with a steam-powered generator. Wartburg Light Corporation purchased an electric plant about 1920. The plant would not produce even one-third the power that it should, so the agent repaid the stockholders about $250 and removed the plant. Wartburg had no electricity. Bruno Schubert offered power plants to individuals for $295 in 1921 and for $525 in 1924. These consisted of internal combustion engines, generators, and batteries. The brand name was Willys Light. Delco-Light was sold by J. E. Lowry of Rockwood, who advertised in the *Morgan County Press*. By 1924 the Citizens Bank, Central High School, and Morgan County Courthouse were all powered by private systems of Willys Light, as were some homes and farms.

Automobiles were first a curiosity, then a convenience, a necessity, and finally a hazard in the county by the 1920s. As early as 1917 J. D. Webster complained in the *Press* about a "reckless" driver from Harriman who passed through Coalfield at 50 miles per hour, demolishing a buggy. He also was concerned about chickens and pigs killed by automobiles and about the noise of auto horns. Little would he have dreamed of the carnage on US 27 in later decades.

The Ford dealer in Rockwood advertised in Morgan County papers as early as 1917. By 1919 Bruno Schubert sold used cars, Morgan County Garage in Wartburg advertised repair service, and Babcock and Son in Sunbright provided repairs. Citizens Motor Company opened in Wartburg in the early 1920s, offering Ford touring cars for $298 and sedans for $595. Sam T. Carr in Oakdale handled Paige and Jewett motor cars. In 1925 Morgan County had 77 automobiles, mostly Fords. By 1930 the county had 694 autos and 92 trucks. The Morgan County Automobile Club organized in Oakdale in 1921 to promote good roads. In 1921 a bus line was established between Knoxville and Wartburg.

In 1920 Wartburg was visted by an "aeroplane."This machine had taken off in Lexington, had run out of gasoline about 10:45 A.M., and had put down on Edel Heidel's farm. Morgan County was now connected to the world by telephone, telegraph, railroad, automobiles, bus lines, and airplanes.

With improved means for travel and with available electricity new leisure-time activities appeared for Morgan County residents and were added to those carried over from the nineteenth century. Secret societies remained—Masons, I.O.O.F, etc.—and fulfilled their functions. Religion was still important. George Moody of Johnson County held a revival in a "canvas tabernacle" in Wartburg which lasted for four weeks in 1924. He was so popular that the *Press* headlined his activities several times and printed his sermons. About 450 persons were converted during the crusade, and $2200 was raised to pay for expenses.

In 1908 the Morgan County Fair had its beginning at Deer Lodge, inspired by a district fair Abner Ross had sponsored there the year before. The county court appropriated $500 and constructed a building for the fair. Crowds arrived on horseback, or in wagons, buggies, and automobiles, bringing their canned products, cakes, candy, bread, crochet, and embroidery to show. The prize specimens of vegetables grown in any year were displayed, and the best livestock in the county shown. A parade inaugurated the fair each year. Costumed children carrying flags, floats decorated according to a theme, decorated automobiles, and of course a queen made up the parade. During the years of World War I patriotic themes were popular. Shows "for men only" occasionally drew criticism in the *Press*.

Towns sponsored community fairs. Sunbright had its fair, and Burrville inaugurated one in 1917. Other types of circulating entertainment appeared in Morgan County each year. The Rose Kilian Musical Comedy Shows, with clowns, jesters, and pantomimists, entertained Wartburg in 1916 with a parade and two shows. The Radcliffe Chautauqua group came to town in the years around 1920, bringing their quality concerts and lectures. Lyceum courses and musical entertainment were also popular in Wartburg during the early twenties.

Baseball was a popular summer activity in the county. Towns sponsored teams, like the Wartburg Grays, which competed with each other. One native of the county, Fred Newberry, who had played for the Wartburg Tigers, was a left-handed pitcher for the Atlanta Crackers and for the New York Yankees.

In the summer of 1923 a movie theater opened in Gobey, a "large roomy house with comfortable seats." Before, movies could only be seen once a year at the county fair, so the opening of the Gobey theater attracted "quite a crowd of Wartburgians."

Moonshining and drinking "white lightning" were popular leisure activities all over the United States in the 1920s, when the Eighteenth Amendment to the Constitution established prohibition. Tennessee had voted dry in 1910, but Morgan County residents were active in the illegal manufacture and sale of alcoholic beverages. In the twelve-month period of 1923 Sheriff Charles W. Human and his deputies raided well over 50 wildcat stills. In January of 1924 he destroyed three stills in four days. He even caught his two nephews making whiskey near their mother's house.

As other apsects of life in Morgan County improved in the first thirty years of the twentieth century, so did the quality of the county's educational system. In 1900 the only school in the county that offered education at the high school level was Mt. Vernon Academy (A. B. Wright Institute) in Burrville. A large number of Morgan County students attended high schools outside the county. Grammar schools usually operated for only about three months each year. The public did not demand longer terms, nor did it support the short terms. In 1903 there were 3869 persons of school age in the county; 2550 enrolled in school that year, but the average daily attendance was only1499. The average salary for teachers was $35.20 per month.

In 1909 the General Assembly passed the General Education Act, providing the first financial support for county high schools. This law generated some agitation for a public high school in Morgan County. In response to the pressure the county court, by vote of 13 to 6, created Morgan County High School and Morgan County High School Board in 1911. The school operated in 1911–1912 at the Odd Fellows Hall in Wartburg. In 1915–1916 Sunbright and Coalfield high schools opened, so Morgan County High School became Central High. Burrville

High School in Wartburg, built in 1924 and burned in 1940. (Courtesy of Charles Kreis)

organized a high school in 1917–1918, and the following year Petros opened one. Oakdale High School started in 1926–1927, and Petros consolidated with Central the same year.

As more schools opened in the 1920s, the county constructed modern buildings. The last log building was used in1915–1916. Brick structures began to appear in 1917–1918. Coalfield received a new three-story building with 17 rooms and an auditorium in 1920. The new building at Sunbright was also dedicated that year. In 1924 a brick building costing $65,000 was finished in Wartburg. It had 11 classrooms, a gymnasium, and an auditorium with 500 seats. It was equipped with steam heat, water, sewage, and showers, and a private system provided electricity. Deer Lodge also received a new building in 1924. All of this expense must have strained the county budget, for in 1924 the rural schools' term was shortened from eight to seven months because of "lack of funds."

The longer terms—nine months for high schools in the 1920s—indicated a more progressive attitude in the county about education, as did the new buildings and improved teacher salaries and training. In 1919 the average salary for elementary teachers was only $55.79 per month, and high school teachers made $70.30. The next year the board of education voted a 20 percent increase for teachers, "the poorest paid class of people in the county." The board also raised its qualifications for teacher training, wanting only teachers "who can make certificate or are normal trained."

When the United States declared war on Germany and the other Central Powers in April of 1917 Morgan County responded patriotically, as it had always done in supporting the nation's wars. The *Press* called September 20, 1917, "one of the great days in the history of Morgan County" when 65 young men departed for military training. A public gathering at the courthouse celebrated the occasion. Students marched from Central High to the courthouse carrying U.S. flags. The crowd sang "America." Prominent citizens made patriotic speeches. Fifteen cheers saluted the Morgan County "sammies." Then citizens with cars decorated in red, white, and blue transported the recruits to the railroad station, giving each man a rose on departure.

Public occasions were opportunities for a show of patriotism during the conflict. A parade at Deer Lodge in the summer of 1917 featured a company of boys with flags, a company of girls decorated with flags, and a figure of America draped in Old Glory and mounted on a horse. The July Fourth celebration in Deer Lodge in 1918 included ladies in Red Cross costumes, Boy Scouts, and a fifty-voice chorus singing patriotic songs.

The county reflected patriotism in its generous donations to funds which financed the war. Only $300 was given to the first Liberty Loan; but in the second the county contributed $8000; and in the third $26,150. The *Press* headlined the fact that the county had oversubscribed the third Liberty Loan by $10,000. To the Red Cross War Fund Morgan County citizens contributed $6657 in 1918—450 percent over the quota.

Patriotism's negative side showed itself in suspicion and prejudice against the German population of Morgan County. There was some pressure on the pastor of St. Paul's Church to discontinue German language services, but they continued until the early twenties. One reader of the *Press* expressed doubt that "the sentiment of the people of Morgan County towards the present war with Germany is as assuring as it should be. . . . If there is one who sympathizes with Germany, . . . let him go to Germany and fight for the Kaiser."

The German population was very loyal toward the United States. Ninety-three of the 110 members of the Morgan County Red Cross chapter during the war were Germans. St. Paul's members contributed $6000 to the third Liberty Loan. Several German boys from the county served in the United States armed forces during the conflict. Henry Kreis was seriously wounded in France.

Two hundred and thirty-three young men had registered for service by the middle of June 1917, and in August ten of these marched off with Company C of the Second Tennessee Regiment. Before the war ended more than 600 had registered for service. Private Joe Nance was the first soldier from Morgan County killed during World War I. By war's end seven had been killed in action, two had been lost at sea, and four had died from illnesses.

When the war was over Morgan County was ready, with the rest of the country, to return to normal times with President Warren G. Harding. The candidate had passed through Morgan County on a train during his campaign in 1920, and the county voted for him in the election. Tennesseans helped put Harding in the White House, the first time that the state had ever voted for a Republican presidental candidate. Alf Taylor, Republican candidate for governor, carried Morgan County and the state.

The Nineteenth Amendment to the Constitution caused a great deal of talk and debate in the nation. Bertha McCartt of Sunbright spoke for Morgan County women: "What women want is equal rights. If women are so essential why are they not capable of running government affairs?" Tennessee's legislature became the pivotal group to ratify the women's suffrage amendment in 1920, but acceptance of the amendment did not quell debate in Morgan County. A Lancing man stated the thoughts of many males: "I have been always opposed to woman suffrage because I knew that they were not physically able to use it. It is not the plan of creation for women to have the franchise." Nevertheless, Morgan County men were not slow in accepting the new status of women, and in 1922 Mrs. A. M. Freytag was elected register of deeds in a race with J. L. Kaufman. "Five orphan children . . . won the election for her," explained the *Press.*

In the 1924 presidential election Morgan County supported Calvin Coolidge, the easy winner; but in the gubernatorial race the county voted for Republican T. F. Peck, who lost to Austin Peay.

Some of the less attractive national trends of the 1920s were reflected in Morgan County during the decade. Violence was all too common. John Barnes tried to shoot Steve Holbert, a cripple, by firing through his house door. Holbert fired back, and both missed. Barnes was arrested. Radicalism was a cause of much violence in the twenties. Finley Melton was shot and killed by a Mrs. Broone in an argument over the "Holly Roller faith." A contractor using black laborers to build the new Coalfield high school in the 1920s disregarded a warning to remove them from town at night. He rented a house for the workers to use, and after only one day of work dynamite was thrown at the house. In 1924 the Ku Klux Klan burned a Catholic church in Deer Lodge. In 1926 the Sunbright KKK met Christmas night in their hall; then they marched to the school and burned a cross.

Charles Darwin's theory of evolution created a great stir in the county. A. B. Peters, superintendent of schools and publisher of the *Morgan County Press,* wrote a "Dear Teacher" letter in his newspaper: "We expect you to condemn socialism and bolshevism and evolution as taught by Darwin, . . . but do it tactfully." The *Press* warned its readers: "There are a few adherents in the county" to Darwinism. "Anyone teaching such a doctrine in our public schools had better stop. . . . The one who teaches it will be put out of school." Darwin's theory "is as dangerous . . . as bolshevism." This controversy was spotlighted in neighboring Rhea County by the famous Scopes trial in 1925. Such a trial might have occurred in Wartburg.

Depression and New Deal

The issues and activities of the Roaring Twenties were overshadowed by the economic depression of the 1930s. With the collapse of the New York Stock Market in October of 1929 the industrial production of the country began to decline and unemployment began to increase. Drought in the early thirties depressed the agricultural economy and more unemployment occurred.

Morgan County suffered along with the rest of the world. Although the population of the county increased by a healthy 1600 during the thirties, some of the towns' populations declined as jobs disappeared. Oakdale was hardest hit because of the decline in railroad traffic during the depression. Its population dropped from 1552 in 1920 to only 900 in 1940. Wartburg's population declined by 100 in the same period. On the other hand, both Petros and Coalfield experienced an increase during the thirties, at least partly because of the prison. Personal economic distress was reflected by the size of the relief rolls. Morgan County had 2842 persons, out of a population of 13,600, on federal relief by January of 1935.

The county government suffered from the economic bite of the depression. In 1935 the county had a large bonded debt, and the tax levy was one of the highest in the state. In 1939 the county court assessed a special tax of 25¢ in order to retire $6000 in outstanding county warrants; but the school fund was also in debt by about $6000, and this was not retired.

The county school system suffered seriously during the thirties. Four high schools operated throughout the decade after Burrville was closed (1931–1932), but there was a pronounced decrease in enrollment. An observer reported that students thought high school had little of value to offer them. One of many problems was the lack of library facilities and services. There was not enough floor space allotted to libraries, books were insufficient in both quantity and quality, and lack of periodicals was the greatest deficiency. No Morgan County high school had a trained librarian. In 1937 slow collection of taxes and lack of federal funds forced elementary schools to close after a seven-month term. The delinquent tax list for the five previous years totaled $101,526.

Another disaster for the school system was the burning of Central High in January of 1940. Originating in a defective flue, the blaze was discovered by students about 11:30 in the morning. They evacuated the building in orderly manner, the student body assuming that they were merely carrying out a fire drill. Since Wartburg had no fire department, the young men at the nearby CCC camp were summoned with their equipment for fighting forest fires. The CCCs managed to save the gymnasium after fighting the fire bravely, but the remainder of the building burned. The loss was estimated at $100,000, with no insurance. This school was reconstructed only in 1945–1946 because of shortages in material and money created by World War II. In the meantime, students went to Sunbright and Oakdale high schools. The old county jail and the Oakdale YMCA also burned in 1940.

With the election of Franklin Roosevelt and his pledge of "a new deal for the American people," hope returned to the land. Morgan County's enthusiasm about FDR was obvious when he stopped at the Oakdale railway station for a few minutes in 1934. More than 1000 hopeful citizens greeted and cheered him. In 1935 his train again stopped at Oakdale for water, but he did not appear. Many spectators had waited in the rain, but this time they were disappointed. In the election of 1936 FDR received 1276 Morgan County votes, to 1139 for Alf Landon. In a 1936 poll of Oakdale students concerning their heros, Roosevelt ranked second after Amelia Earhart, but higher than Charles Lindbergh and Henry Ford.

Roosevelt's New Deal played a significant part in the economic life of Morgan County. Although the county continued to maintain its poor list—persons who were voted "on" or "off" the list by the county court and received payments of $10 to $15 per quarter—the burden of handling unemployment was assumed by the state and federal governments in the thirties. The Tennessee Welfare Department had 291 aged clients in Morgan

County in 1939–1940 who received $30,761. The Department of Public Welfare gave financial aid to 211 children in 89 families in the county in that fiscal year.

Morgan County was quick to benefit from work programs that the New Deal offered. In 1933 the county requested $54,000 to repair the courthouse and schools and to improve the county's highways. In 1935 some of that money was forthcoming—funds to employ 59 men to work on the courthouse and 132 men to work on the roads. In 1935 the WPA provided an additional $145,371 for road improvement. New Deal money also helped pay teachers' salaries, some of it designated as back pay.

The Civilian Conservation Corps provided an important employment opportunity for young men in the county. Company 1463, Camp S-79, was established in Morgan State Forest near Flat Fork Creek in 1933, but after two months in this location the tent camp moved to a site two miles west of Wartburg, where barracks were constructed. In 1937 the camp moved back into Morgan State Forest and remained there until it closed in 1940. Approximately 150 young men enrolled in Camp S-79.

Only young men, age 18 to 25, enrolled in the CCC. The Corps was under the command of the U.S. Army; the young men wore uniforms and lived by military regulations. Pay was $30 a month, which seemed like a lot of money to them. The work was manual labor under the direction of the forest service.

Numerous young men from Morgan County enrolled in the CCC, and many of them served at Camp S-79. Others had their first opportunity to travel; they were sent by the Corps to camps in other parts of Tennessee and in other states. One Morgan County boy served in Utah, and some went to the West Coast; after Camp S-79 closed in 1940 many Morgan County boys went to the camps at Norris and Crossville. Recruits from other counties and states served in the Morgan County camp. Some of them married Morgan County girls and settled there. The CCC created a movement of population both in and out of the county.

Life at the camp was a positive experience for the young men. Many received more and better food than they had eaten at home. Many acquired useful skills, and the general broadening experience of traveling and communicating with people had positive effects. Three men died from accidents while working in Camp S-79. One was crushed by a boulder, one killed in an explosion, and one crushed in a truck wreck.

Camp S-79 boys worked in several surrounding counties, fighting forest fires, building fire control towers, stringing telephone lines between towers and towns, constructing truck and horse trails, and erecting a few buildings. The workers used trucks and bulldozers, but most of the labor was hand work.

The CCC provided emergency aid in Wartburg on two occasions. In 1935 the business district caught fire late on a Sunday night in May. Since Wartburg had no fire department and no water system, the CCC camp was notified, and the boys came with their fire fighting equipment. A hardware store, a law office, and the post office burned; Citizens Bank suffered damage. The CCC camp also fought the Central High fire in 1940.

The CCC camp conducted classes in vocational, academic, and agricultural subjects, and offered practical instruction in health, safety, and citizenship. Sports were a part of camp life; S-79 won a baseball championship in 1936 and a field meet in 1937. It was selected as the best camp in District C in April of 1937.

After the CCC camp closed Morgan County entered the National Youth Administration program. In 1941 the county court voted $1000 to match NYA money to build a workshop at Central High. The shop provided vocational training for youths aged 16 to 23.

Two permanent programs of the New Deal affected Morgan County toward the end of the decade. The Social Security Act of 1935 made its first payments in 1937; eleven persons in Morgan County received checks. Farmers Home Administration made its first loans in the county in 1940.

Two New Deal programs which eventually affected everyone in Morgan County were the Tennessee Valley Authority and the Rural Electrification Administration. Tennessee Electric Power Company had provided electricity to parts of the county in the early 1930s and advertised its rates and its appliances in the *Morgan County News.* In 1936 the county court gave TVA permission to extend lines into the county, an REA committee was appointed, and TVA took an option on TEP lines. In 1939 TVA proposed an electric co-op for Morgan and Scott counties, to be called Plateau Electric Co-operative. REA would lend money for the lines and the power would be bought from Tennessee Electric Power in Harriman. Five hundred co-op members were to be recruited, each paying a $5 fee. The cooperative was organized and 502 residents joined by the end of 1941. Plateau Electric borrowed $230,000 for construction of lines, but materials were not available because of the war preparations.

The New Deal was beneficial to farmers in Morgan County. The Soil Conservation and Domestic Allotment Act of 1936 allowed payments to persons who withdrew land from cultivation and practiced soil conservation measures on it. Morgan County had 400 farmers in the program in its first year who received $12,000; by 1938 there were more than 1000 participating. This number was nearly 100 percent of the farmers in the county.

In 1934 Morgan County produced a record crop of white potatoes, 125,000 bushels worth $75,000; potatoes became the major cash crop for the county in the thirties. By the end of the decade the county was third in the state in the amount of potatoes grown. During the war the government asked that Morgan County produce 200,000 bushels in one year, but this unrealistic goal could not be reached. Morgan County was 4th in the number of apple trees in the state, and was 28th in sheep raising. Agricultural leaders were very disappointed in sheep production, for Morgan County had an ideal ecology for this stock. In 1936 there were only 63,000 pounds of wool in the wool pool, and by 1939 it had declined to 4000 pounds.

The industrial economy of Morgan County profited little from the New Deal. Manufacturing was not encouraged, but natural resources were extracted. Over 500 men were involved in timber enterprises in 1940, and over 400 in coal mining. Petroleum production employed a number of men, and there was a brick plant in Oliver Springs.

Lancing in the twentieth century. Note the railroad station at left, Walt house behind, post office in center, general store, mail hook at right, and load of pulpwood on the track. (Courtesy of Charles Kreis)

Six lumber companies in the county harvested hundreds of acres of timber each year; forest fires destroyed thousands more. In addition to natural and accidental causes of fire, county residents were also responsible for many fires. Farmers burned pasture and wood in the early spring to encourage the grass to grow earlier for their stock. These fires destroyed timber as well as dead grass. In the 1930s Morgan County had one of the highest fire rates in the state—about 15 percent of all the state's forest fires. In the spring of 1935 there were 86 forest fires in a month; by the middle of July 200 fires had been counted. In 1936, 451 fires burned 36,000 acres and cost $98,000. Of the total number, 312 were thought to be incendiary.

Another concern with Morgan's forests in the 1930s was the sale of thousands of acres of Rugby's virgin stands to lumber companies. In 1939 the Webb Lumber Company of Oneida bought some of Rugby's land, including the townsite. Outrage at the possibility of denuding the terrain and destroying the historic colony was widespread. Editors of prestigious newspapers like the *New York Times* and the *Washington Post* raised their voices against the carnage. Some timber was cut, but the town was saved.

Coal and oil production continued in the county. Both gas wells and oil wells were drilled, and strip mining was practiced as a quick and inexpensive means of extracting coal. Tennessee Valley Collieries Company produced 2500 tons per week from its Morgan County strip mine, the largest such operation in Tennessee in 1944. It employed 26 men and operated 24 hours per day.

Brushy Mountain Penitentiary continued to be an important catalyst for Morgan County's economy. The prison and the railroad associated with it provided employment and income for many residents of the area. In 1936 there were 62 employees at the prison; 46 of these were guards. Salaries of the employees were low. The warden's annual income was only $1800 with maintenance, and guards made $720 with maintenance and $840 without. This was considered too low by the Tennessee State Planning Commission; nevertheless it provided an economic boost for the area, particularly during the depression period.

The number of inmates in the prison continually increased. In 1926 there were 478 inmates, but by 1931 the number was 975. The building would accommodate only three or four hundred men, so double use was made of the cells. The day shift for the mines arose at 5:00 A.M., ate breakfat, and rode to the mines in railroad carts. Their work shift continued until 4:30 P.M. The night shift arose at 2:00 P.M., worked from 5:30 P.M. to 7:00 A.M. and had breakfast at 7:30. Sunday was a day of no work, with visiting hours from 8:00 A.M. to 4:00 P.M.

In addition to work in the mines, some prisoners labored on the farm, which originally consisted of 60 acres. By 1937 the state farmed 200 acres, leased on a sharecrop basis from private landowners. Thousands of pounds of beans, tomatoes, and apples grown on the farm were preserved for prison use in a cannery built in the compound in 1934.

Most of the prison's total acreage changed management in 1933 when 9000 acres of the mountainous area around the compound were transferred to the Department of Agriculture. This area had been logged about 1920, and it now was dotted with only poor second-growth timber. Named Morgan State Forest,

Brushy Mountain Penitentiary, Petros, built 1933-34. (Courtesy of Tennessee State Library and Archives)

it served as the living and work area for the CCC camp discussed above.

In 1931 a legislative committee reported on the condition of Brushy Mountain Penitentiary facilities. They "approach conditions which prevailed in the Siberian prisons under the old Russian regime." The prison was "a most dangerous fire hazard." The committee concluded that conditions were "indefensible and should not be tolerated" and recommended fireproof barracks with sanitary facilities and an adequate hospital. If the state would not correct these intolerable conditions, then Brushy Mountain should be closed and sold.

In 1933 excavation and construction on a new building began in front of and to the right of the old structure. The New Deal supplied 150 Civil Works Administration laborers for three or four months, but inmates did most of the work. The new building was to be built from stone quarried nearby, with convicts supplying the labor; but this procedure was too slow and reinforced concrete was substituted.

J. N. Brooks, supervisor of construction for state institutions, designed the new building on the plan of a Greek cross, with two bars of equal length crossing each other at right angles. It was three stories high with four levels of cells to accommodate 630 men. The two cell blocks in the right and left wings of the structure were segregated into white and black areas. Each cell had a double deck bunk, a washbasin, and a commode. The front wing of the building contained administrative offices, and the rear wing contained offices, kitchens, and dining rooms.

The structure was complete in January of 1935 at a cost of only $45,960; it was valued at $176,000. Money for the facility came from the Tennessee Industrial Division, a revolving fund made up of unexpended funds from state institutions. A report in 1937 by the Tennessee State Planning Commission indicated that living conditions at Brushy Mountain were still undesirable. Four inmates lived in the new cells built to house two men; two would sleep in the cell while the other two were on work shift. The cells were dirty, as were the bathrooms and the hospital. Three hundred men were still in the old wooden building, part of which remained after the new building was constructed. The old buildings and equipment were "filthy," and the facility was condemned as "totally unsuited for human habitation."

During the decade of the depression Americans sought entertainment and pleasure as leisure activity and as escape from economic woes. One of the most popular forms of entertainment during this time, because it was new and because it was inexpensive, was the movie theater. The Princess Theater in Harriman and the theater in Gobey offered films. *Trail of the Lonesome Pine,* screened at the Princess in 1936, was the first all-color movie to be shown in the area. Movies were also shown in the Central High School building during the thirties. The *Morgan County News* carried both movie reviews and stories about movie stars' lives on its front pages.

School and church plays, religious revivals, and fairs were still parts of Morgan County's leisure-time activities. Wartburg and other towns held community fairs in the later thirties and early forties. Maybe for this reason among others, the Morgan County Fair at Deer Lodge began to decline during the depression years. In 1935 the fairgrounds were offered for sale, and the fair was not revived until after World War II.

Although the United States repealed the Eighteenth Amendment in 1933 and returned liquor options to the states, Morgan County remained officially dry during the depression. In 1937 a vote for legal sales of liquor in the county failed to pass—567 voting dry and 183 voting wet. Three years later the wets won by a 35 vote margin, but the election commission discovered that some ballots had been stolen from the school superintendent's office. Annadel turned in 50 wet votes and 3 dry votes even though it had held no liquor election. So those votes were discounted and the drys won, 541–533. Oakdale did allow Oakdale Liquor to open in 1940—"on the highway." Illegal whiskey was available during the depression, and Sheriff Brock seized 116 stills in 30 months.

World War II and Postwar Progress

The war which followed the Japanese bombing of Pearl Harbor in December of 1941 brought the depression to an end. Production soared, unemployment disappeared, prices were controlled, and Americans' minds turned from individual and national problems to the military problems in Asia and Europe.

Morgan County, with its usual patriotic spirit, turned out to support the war. No one questioned the loyalty of the county's Germans in this war. Clarence Connant, a soldier from Oliver Springs, was wounded in the attack on Pearl Harbor. Morgan County draftees left for Fort Oglethorpe in Georgia in July of 1941. The first Morgan County casualty, Rex G. Boardman from Lancing, died when U.S.S. *Langley* sank in the Indian Ocean in 1942.

The county produced and economized for the war effort. In a campaign to gather scrap aluminum, collection points were announced in the *News*. Iron scrap drives started and the county agent urged farmers to increase production of "vital defense foods." The Morgan County Agricultural Defense Board was created, and the United States asked the county to double the production of potatoes.

Rationing was mandated. A county tire rationing board functioned, and rationing of meat, sugar, gas, shoes, and processed foods ensued. The WPA School Lunch, Gardening and Food Preservation Project provided for the growing, processing, and serving of food in school lunch programs.

Financial drives were successful. The Red Cross War Fund collected $2200 in early 1942. Post offices sold war bonds, and school children were urged to save their dimes and buy.

Cheesecake photos of Hollywood starlets appeared on the front pages of the *News,* as did draftee lists, awards to soldiers, letters from soldiers, and casualty lists. One soldier sent the *News* photos of three Japanese soldiers he had killed.

By 1945, 65 Morgan Countians had given their lives in the war. They were honored in the American Legion War Memorial Building constructed in Wartburg after the war.

After the New Deal period and World War II, Morgan County voted Democratic, like other parts of the country. In 1948 the county supported Harry Truman by a narrow margin and voted for Democrat Gordon Browning for governor. Browning, emphasizing rural roads and education in his administration, visited Morgan County twice during his two terms. On one of these occasions he spoke to a teachers' meeting, supporting the county's campaign for an east-west highway. The contract on Highway 62 was let in 1949. Morgan County gratefully supported Browning for a third consecutive term in 1952 when Frank Clement defeated him in the primary.

Morgan County residents gave little notice to the Korean War's first year—1950. In the next year Red Cross Fund notices appeared, but the campaign to raise money was not as enthusiastic as in World War II. The first Morgan County soldier died in 1951. That same year Cpl. George Googe, a 22-year-old machine gunner from Coalfield, was hailed by local papers as the Army's "top killer." President Eisenhower ended the conflict in 1953, by which time five Morgan County soldiers had lost their lives.

In 1952 Morgan County voted heavily for the Republican presidential candidate, Dwight Eisenhower, as did the state and the nation; but in the gubernatorial race the county supported Democratic candidate Clement just as strongly.

The new governor shocked Morgan County citizens by removing Floyd Freytag as warden at Brushy Mountain Prison. Freytag, who owned Plateau Tractor and Implement Company in Wartburg, was well-known and popular as warden. He had used prisoners for work on schoolhouses, churches, county fair buildings, roads, and cemeteries in the county. In his place Governor Clement appointed Bob Evans as temporary manager, then Frank Llewellyn as permanent warden. In March of 1958 a two-day riot at the prison caused serious problems. A columnist in the *News* attributed it to incompetent administration at the prison and blamed Clement for not correcting the problems.

In the 1958 gubernatorial race the county narrowly supported Buford Ellington, Clement's commissioner of agriculture. Freytag commented in the *News* that Ellington would be governor for four years "whether we like it or not." More citizens in the county had voted for the other two candidates, McCord and Wall, than for Ellington.

In the 1960s the voters supported Richard Nixon in two presidential elections and Lyndon Johnson in the third. On the local scene politics swirled around the question of municipal incorporation in the county's towns. Wartburg had been incorporated in the nineteenth century, but this was repealed in 1891, upon petition from its citizens. After World War II Oakdale was the only incorporated municipality in the county. Wartburg held a vote on incorporation in 1963. The *News* campaigned in favor of it, while opponents raised the issue of increased taxes. Supporters answered with promises of an improved water system, a sewer system, and more industry. Interest in the question was great, for 310 of 360 qualified voters cast ballots. One hundred and eighty-four voted against incorporation; 126 voted in favor. Sunbright held a vote concerning incorporation in 1966 and also turned it down, 183 to 98.

In 1968 Wartburg tried again. This time the area of incorporation was smaller than in 1963. Two hundred and seventeen citizens voted, and the results were heavily in favor of incorporation—154 "yes" votes and 63 "no" votes. Roy McNeal was elected the first mayor later in the year.

After three years as an incorporated town, Wartburg reviewed the results with satisfaction in 1971. The town collected no city tax, but received all its revenue from sales tax and gas tax; it had a $5308 positive balance at the end of 1971. After three years the town had added some street lights, collected garbage in some areas, and hired a night patrolman.

When World War II ended Morgan County and the rest of the country wanted to recreate the good life that had been interrupted by depression and war. The soldiers returning to civilian life and the civilians waiting for them to return were all ready for better and happier times.

The revived county fair was one sign of a return to the good life. The fair, which had closed during the depression, reopened in 1949 on rented land, using a tent to house the exhibits. In 1951 the county purchased a fairground, and the next year a permanent exhibit building was constructed. By 1956 buildings valued at $50,000 had been put up. Several towns in the county revived their community fairs in the early 1950s. By 1967, however, the county fair had declined to such a point that a *News* editorial pronounced it an "unjustified expenditure." The county had subsidized the fair with $2500 in 1967, yet fewer people attended, and they were greeted by empty exhibit stalls. The fair continued, however, and in 1978 the thirtieth annual fair was celebrated.

One popular form of entertainment after the war was the movie. Four theaters operated in Morgan County and Harriman in the 1950s. The Princess and the Webbo in Harriman, the Pioneer in Wartburg, and the Dixie Drive-In in Sunbright offered the latest in Hollywood fare.

Legal alcohol and illegal bootleg were available in the county due to the demand of returning soldiers who had been exposed to different cultures in other parts of the world. By 1950 Morgan County had 17 bars which sold beer; but when the local option referendum for liquor was presented to the voters in 1953, it was overwhelmingly defeated—2467 to 388. In 1974 Wartburg City Council approved beer sales for that town.

Illegal liquor was obviously still available and still popular. Sheriff Claude Brasel captured 73 stills in four years during the 1950s. Sheriff Cecil R. Byrge found and destroyed two 500-gallon stills and a 250-gallon still around 1970. In 1972 about two dozen marijuana plants were found growing in a home near Deer Lodge; the owner was arrested. Eighty plants were found at Deer Lodge the next month, and 85 plants in Catoosa.

Frozen Head Natural Area, with more than 10,000 acres, became a recreation area in the county in the early seventies. This land was originally part of the prison property, and then became Morgan State Forest. A region of great natural beauty, the park had housed the CCC camp in the 1930s, during which time the workers had constructed some roads and a bridge, 75 miles of trail, and a cabin in the park. In 1971 the Division of State Parks improved the roads and built picnic tables, cooking grills, water fountains, a picnic shelter, and a toilet building. Not only does this beautiful park serve the residents of Morgan County; more importantly, it brings other people seeking recreation into the county.

In Rugby, 20 of the original Victorian buildings still stand. The schoolhouse is now a visitor center and guided walking tours are given daily through Christ Church, Episcopal, the Thomas Hughes Free Public Library, and Hughes's home, Kingstone Lisle. Historic Rugby hosts two special events each year: the Spring Music and Crafts Festival in May and the Rugby Pilgrimage of Homes in August. Near this rural village in a rugged river gorge setting state parks and a new national recreational area offer rafting, hiking, horseback riding, camping, and other outdoor activities.

REA plans to run power lines into Morgan County had been suspended by the outbreak of World War II, but immediately after the war the projects were resumed. Electric lines were to be strung into the county from various points by different power companies. Coalfield was to be serviced by Clinton Power, south

Morgan County by Harriman Power, and the Pine Orchard area by Rockwood Power. Plateau Electric Co-op was to run lines through Lancing, Deer Lodge, Burrville, and Rugby. It was hoped that these plans would take electric power to practically every family in Morgan County; but this was not to be. An irate citizen, in a letter to the *News* in 1948, claimed that only 800 of the almost 16,000 residents of the county had electricity. Deer Lodge, Burrville, and Flat Fork had no power from Plateau Electric. In 1949 Plateau Electric corrected the problem and quieted the complaints. The co-op board borrowed more than $1,000,000 from the government to build 320 miles of line and add 2800 members to its system. By 1950 the county had electric power in all its sections, and this service provided a basis for the good life to all the residents. Now many could purchase the appliances and machines that made American life the envy of the world. All the basic home appliances were available in area stores. Even the newest luxury, 21-inch black and white television sets, were available for $159.95.

City water systems and sewer systems were installed in the county after the war. Wartburg was first with the Plateau Utility District in 1954. By December two 300-foot wells had been drilled to provide the water; pipes followed. Other towns built water and sewer systems, using federal money in the sixties and seventies.

In a number of important ways the agricultural economy changed in Morgan County after World War II. Most obvious was a decline in the number of farms, from 1632 in 1940 to 559 in 1964. This was common in the state and throughout the country. Farm prices were not as high after the war, and the industrial economy pulled labor away from the farms. Those who continued to live on farms after the war, and some of those who lived in town and owned farms, were only part-time farmers. Fifty-six percent of farmers in the county worked at nonfarm jobs during 1964, increasing their income by $3497 per family. The total income of farmers from nonfarm work exceeded their income from farm products.

The federal government provided financial aid for the farmers, continuing the first farm programs initiated by the New Deal before the war. Henry Wattenbarger, county supervisor for the Farmers Home Administration, directed government loans to farmers. Money for puchasing farms, seeding pasture, and improving soil and water resources was available. FmHA loans financed purchases of livestock and machinery, and construction of homes and barns. The agency made hundreds of loans in Morgan and Scott counties. A severe drought in 1955 brought federal emergency loans to Morgan County farmers. In the same year the worst rains since 1929 damaged farm lands, roads, bridges, and businesses.

In a change from earlier trends, livestock was the most profitable aspect of farming after the war. The potential that early settlers in Wartburg and Rugby had failed to realize was accomplished by Morgan County farmers 100 years later. Livestock sales accounted for 76 percent of all farm income in 1964, with poultry sales being the largest single source of income. The quality of beef cattle improved, with a number of registered herds and blooded bulls brought in. Six new dairies were established in 1956, improving another potential for the county economy. Swine, sheep, and goat production continued to decline after the war.

Crop sales accounted for only 24 percent of farm income in 1964. Tobacco was the single most valuable crop, with 72,716 pounds harvested in 1960. Potatoes, strawberries, beans, and fruits were important cash crops; grains were produced in varying amounts for livestock food. Farmers still grew more corn, although wheat production increased; rye declined.

Immediately after World War II there was no manufacturing in Morgan County; industrial production was still confined to processing natural resources. In 1949 the Tennessee Directory of Manufacturers listed two lumber companies and a coal mine in Sunbright, a lumber company and a coal mine for Oakdale, and no industry for any other town. In that year Brys Ceramic Studio and Varga Woodcraft opened in Sunbright; three more lumber companies opened in 1950.

In the 1950s both the Morgan County Industrial Development Council and the Morgan County Quarterly Court Industrial Development Committee operated to encourage and attract industry. In 1962 the county court had created the Industrial Development Board to promote development of rural areas, and in 1964 the District One Development Organization was formed to promote the Coalfield area.

In addition to this plethora of committees and boards, the county offered some tangible enticements to industry. In 1961 the voters approved $200,000 in industrial revenue bonds; the *News* had campaigned enthusiastically in favor of the bonds. In 1965 bids were let for two buildings to be constructed with county money. One structure in Wartburg was occupied by the Tennessee Woven Label Company, and the second in Sunbright was used by the Frank Williams Corporation to expand the Sunbright Shirt Factory.

In another move to attract industry, in 1962 the county court voted 14 to 10 to employ an industrial plant specialist to conduct a search for industry. Taxes were increased 15¢ in order to pay the agent's $12,000 salary. Only two applicants appeared for the position, and no one had been employed by the end of the year. In 1963 Eugene McDonald, president of the Scott County Chamber of Commerce, accepted the position. By 1966 he had been instrumental in acquiring five plants for the county, which created 975 jobs and a $4,000,000 payroll.

In 1967 Morgan County joined a consortium of 16 counties to promote the economic development of the area. The General Assembly had chartered the East Tennessee Development District in 1966, which was headquartered on the University of Tennessee campus in Knoxville. Seventy-five percent of its funds were to be federal grants and loans. In the next 15 years the ETDD completed over 200 projects. In Morgan County the organization aided with water system loans and grants for Sunbright and Oakdale and with sewer and gas loans and grants for Wartburg. In 1973 the county purchased 100 acres of land on the prison farm and developed it into an industrial park.

Morgan County's efforts to attract industry in the fifties and sixties were successful. Sunbright Shirt Company opened in

1960, employing 50 workers to manufacture boys' shirts. By 1964 it was using 90–100 workers. Tennessee Woven Label Company opened in Wartburg in 1965, employing 13. In that year the county court exempted these two factories and Dyna Tex Corporation from county taxes. This obvious attempt to satisfy these industries and attract more was criticized by the editor of the *News,* who inveighed against such concessions.

In 1967 Morgan Apparel, an affiliate of Red Kap of Nashville, opened in Wartburg to manufacture men's work shirts. It was to employ well over 100. Kellwood Company of St. Louis, employing over 100 laborers to make boys' shirts, replaced the Sunbright Shirt Company. By 1970 industry was a significant employer in Morgan County. Eight hundred and thirty-eight persons were employed in textiles and 210 in furniture factories. Only 137 worked in mines and 163 in chemicals. In attracting textile manufacturers Morgan County was similar to other parts of the state. All but about ten of the state's 95 counties had at least one clothing manufacturing firm in the 1970s; this industry was Tennessee's leading employer. It did not demand much training or education, neither did it pay high wages; but it did provide work.

Many Morgan Countians worked outside the county. Lumber, coal, and railroads employed fewer workers after the war, and the manufacturing industry could not absorb them all. More than 1000 people worked in other counties in 1960, most of them in Roane or Anderson counties. Only 1944 industrial laborers worked in Morgan County that year. By 1980 about as many residents worked outside as inside the county.

One industrial disappointment for the county was the failure of the Dyna Tex plant. Talks started between county officials and representatives of the firm in 1964. The county offered tax exemption in 1965 and agreed to provide $260,000 in start-up funds. In return Dyna Tex, owned by Holiday Inns, was to build a plant in Sunbright to manufacture particle board. It was to employ hundreds of workers and consume 200 cords of pulpwood a day. The firm secured an Area Redevelopment Administration loan of $1,693,000 and constructed a building, but the

Railroad tunnel construction in the 1960s. (Courtesy of Charles Kreis)

plant never went into production. After some delay in receiving and installing machinery purchased in Europe, the plant employed about 100 workers and then closed in April of 1970. Holiday Inns explained that the plant could never produce enough particle board to show a profit. The county entertained some hope of securing another operator, but this did not develop.

Railroads provided some economic input for the county after the war, but their economic importance declined as they were replaced by trucks and planes. Beginning in 1961 five railroad tunnels in Morgan County were eliminated, enlarged, or relocated. This provided some employment and economic activity; but also in 1961 the railroad started to close stations in Morgan County. Sunbright lost its station and agent in May of 1961, and railroad officials announced later in the year that Oakdale would close. That station's expenses for nine months were $8474, and its revenues were only $369. The station was not closed, however, until 1967 and 1969, when passenger service north and south was terminated. The time when the railroad was an important economic catalyst for the county had passed.

Some economic advances for the county in the 1970s included the expansion of Red Kap in Wartburg, with the employment of 100 additional workers. Blue Hole Canoe Company opened in Sunbright in 1976. The woven labels factory in Wartburg was employing 120 people by 1978. Deerlodge Industries, opened in 1973, employed 65 people by 1978 to manufacture men's trousers. Kellwood in Sunbright was working 250 people by 1978. That year, 867 workers were employed in six other plants in Morgan County.

In 1981 North American Philips Corporation opened Advance Transformer to manufacture coils for microwave ovens and employed 300 laborers. This was an important change in Morgan County's industrial development, which to this time had been confined almost entirely to textiles.

The older industries of Morgan County, those which extracted natural resources, continued to utilize labor and produce wealth, but they were not as large a part of the county's economy after the war. In 1947 there were 47 lumber mills, and as late as 1965 Morgan County produced more pulpwood than any county in Tennessee. In 1960 the wood industry—including lumber, furniture, and wood products—employed 335 laborers, more than any other single industry in the county. This was to decline in the next two decades. In 1976 the total income for forest products was less than $500,000 per year. The forest service thought it could be developed to at least $2 million annually.

Coal mining, which employed 306 persons in 1960, was already in a decline. The large Mahan-Ellison Mines closed in 1955; coal production in the county decreased for the next ten years. Fourteen coal companies still operated in the county in 1965, but by 1970 only 137 workers were employed. By the mid-1970s strip mining was more prevalent than underground mining, and this damaged Morgan County's greatest resource—its natural beauty.

Oil and gas production were now more important than coal as an employer. In 1960 there were 150 people working in this industry, and in 1970 there were 163. A total of 48 wells in the county had produced since the first was drilled; about 95 had been drilled. The first well after the war was drilled in 1947, and within twenty years about a dozen wells were producing oil and gas. In 1973 a well which produced both oil and gas was drilled. The *News* claimed that it might be the most productive well east of the Mississippi River. In 1979 another new well produced about 5000 barrels in one day.

Nevertheless, unemployment and poverty remained substantial in the 1960s and 1970s. President Lyndon Johnson's Great Society program, updating FDR's New Deal, attempted to address these problems.

The Neighborhood Youth Corps, obviously an agency close to the President's heart because he had been head of the National Youth Administration in Texas in the 1930s, was organized in Morgan County in 1965. The Corps spent $29,330 that year to employ more than 100 young persons during the summer.

Head Start, a learning program to upgrade educational prospects for underprivileged children, received $38,023 in 1965. By 1968 the program enrolled 200 children in ten schools in the county. The Elementary and Secondary Education Act of 1965 put $190,000 into the school system in that year.

An attempt to upgrade the lives of the lower economic groups as well as to benefit local merchants resulted in the food stamp program. Morgan County had 279 families on the program in January of 1967, and the county court expressed concern about lost dollars because more families did not participate. By October there were 1996 participants. In 1973 over 20 percent (2869 persons) of the county's population was enrolled in the program.

Heavy construction projects that federal money financed improved life in the county. In the early 1960s an airport sponsored by Rockwood and Roane County was placed in Morgan County because of land configuration. It was to be financed by a federal grant and by bond money from Roane County and Rockwood. Roane County voted against the bond, but Morgan County Court donated $5000 to the project. Oakdale gave $2500 to the airport. Eventually Rockwood raised the most money to match state and federal funds for the airport, which cost $800,000.

Fowler Field was dedicated in November of 1962. Southern Airways promised to fly three daily flights in and out. After three years of service, Southern terminated flights to Fowler Field in 1966 and transferred its service to the Crossville airport. Today Fowler Field is open only to private planes.

Several towns in Morgan County benefitted from the Great Society. Sunbright was granted $135,000 in 1961 for a new waterworks system; Wartburg received $137,000 in 1963; and Oakdale received $445,000 in 1968. In 1970 Wartburg obtained a very large grant, over $1,000,000 from various agencies, for a sewer and gas system. The county officials occupied a new federal building in Wartburg in 1970, housing the post office, the selective service, the Farmers Home Administration, the extension service, and the soil conservation service.

In 1974 Morgan County received $222,168 in federal revenue sharing funds. In 1975 East Tennessee Development District announced that the county had obtained $578,977 through its agency over the past two years.

With the aid of the generally prosperous economy of the fifties and sixties, and with the additional boost of Great Society programs, Morgan County was able to achieve some economic advances after the war. By 1970, however, with the nation's economy struggling with both inflation and depression, and with the Great Society programs being strangled by conservative reaction, the national economy began to suffer. In addition, Morgan County faced another problem which the nation as a whole did not share.

Unlike the rest of the nation, Morgan County's population began to decline after World War II. The peak was recorded in the 1950 census at 15,727, and by 1960 it had dropped to 14,304. In 1970 it was 13,619. This trend was reversed in the 1980 census, with the county showing an impressive gain to 16,829. Morgan County had suffered from the general out-migration from rural areas to urban areas in the nation.

After World War II, when materials and labor were again

available, Morgan County constructed a number of new school buildings. Central High was rebuilt in 1945–1946, and again in 1956 because of an unsatisfactory roof. Burrville School had burned in 1949; in 1950 its new building was completed. Contracts were let for schools in Sunbright and Lancing in 1950 and for Pine Orchard in 1951. In 1961 the Deer Lodge elementary school, a four-room brick structure, burned after a muffled explosion. Sheriff H. E. Byrge, certain that the building had been doused with gasoline, offered a reward for the arsonist; no one was ever convicted. The school was rebuilt the following year.

Federal funds poured into Morgan County's school system after the war. The first money, in 1957, was $20,401 from the US Office of Education. This program paid $79.90 per individual for children of federal workers going to school in the county; Morgan County had 301 such students. School cafeterias received USDA surplus food after the war to supplement their lunch programs.

By 1960 school enrollment had begun to drop, paralleling the decline in the county's population. In the seventies enrollment fluctuated, and in 1979 the school system had 3450 students. In the 1960s the county spent $301 per student, more than Roane and Cumberland, but less than the average for Tennessee ($321). Morgan County had 155 teachers, and 55 of these had less than the batchelor's degree. This was a higher percentage than Roane and Cumberland counties, and much higher than the Tennessee average (13 percent).

In the 1970s the county put additional money into its education system. The Petros-Joyner school building opened in 1976. The Morgan County Vocational Center, also opened that year, trained high school students in skills which would enable them to contribute to the county's economic growth. In 1978 the school board approved an $8.5 million renovation program for all the county's schools. Voters authorized bonds to finance the renovation but the county commissioners refused to issue them. In 1980 a two-cent sales tax passed to fund the renovation—the first county sales tax. In November the commission agreed to the renovation program because the state threatened to cut off school funds.

Morgan County had to struggle to maintain adequate health care facilities and services for its population after 1945. In its earlier history the area had been blessed with medical doctors. Wartburg had a multitude of physicians in the nineteenth century and through the first half of the twentieth century. As late as 1940 three medical doctors advertised their services in the town.

After the war the situation became serious, and the people of the county were concerned. "Morgan County has been losing doctors recently," commented the *News* in 1953. The reason given for this problem was that the county did not have a hospital or a health center. Lacking the financial means to build a hospital, the county court voted $25,000 to build a health center building and attract a physician. Constructed in 1954, the center attracted both a physician and a dentist. Dr. Paul McCammon agreed to head the medical staff at the center, and Dr. William H. Piper would practice as a dentist. By 1957 Dr. McCammon had departed, and Dr. Edgar Akin moved into the medical center. Dr. Sam Jones was practicing medicine in Sunbright. In 1965 there were only two doctors in the entire county, and after 1966 there were no practicing physicians.

In 1969 a new medical center was built on the campus of Central High School. The facility cost $100,000, most of which was a grant from the federal government. Dr. Hugo John Cole practiced in the clinic for some time, but in 1973 the county had to appeal to the National Health Service to supply it with physicians. Two doctors came to the county to serve two-year terms of service. They were employees of, and paid by, the National Health Service.

In the 1970s Morgan County was still far behind in supplying health services for its population, as was the entire Cumberland Plateau. By 1979 Morgan County had four physicians practicing for a population of almost 17,000. Petros and Deer Lodge opened health centers to augment the one in Wartburg. The county still had no hospital.

Despite the improvement and diversification of Morgan County's economy after 1945, residents of the county were not able to match income gains in other parts of the state and nation. The median family income in Morgan County in 1959 was $2308, far below the US median of $5660. The poverty line income was $3000 in 1959, and 61.1 percent of Morgan County's population fell below this line. By 1969 the county's median family income had increased to $5363, but it was still one of the poorer counties in East Tennessee. The *News* was happy to report in 1973 that 44.8 percent of the county's population earned over $5000 a year, compared to only 36 percent in 1969. By 1979 the median family income had increased significantly to $12,331. Morgan County had made significant economic progress since 1959.

The tax income of the county declined in the 1960s because of lower receipts from the railroad. Morgan County depended to an enormous extent on the railroad tax to meet its budget. In 1960 the railroad paid 57 percent of all taxes collected in the county. The railroad's assessment was lowered at this time, so the individual tax rate in the county had to be increased. The new tax rate in 1960 was $5, up 70¢ from the year before. This must have been a financial shock to county residents, but it was necessary to replace lost railroad revenue. In 1961 the rate increased to $5.21 to build a new school at Deer Lodge, and in 1962 the rate was $5.45 to pay the salary of the industrial recruiter. The high rate of $6.90 was assessed in 1968 to pay for $80,000 lost in reduced railroad taxes over a two-year period. The next year the rate dropped to $4.90, and by 1973 it was down to $2.90. In 1978 the tax climbed back to $7.55, the highest tax rate in the state. This increased rate was also brought about by lowered assessments on the railroad. The county approved a one-cent increase in the sales tax to cover the losses, and in 1979 the property tax dropped to $ 4.20.

Brushy Mountain Prison, with its problems, hurt the county's economy. In 1966 the last prison-operated coal mine closed, the mine entrance sealed with a dynamite blast. The mine was unsafe, the coal supply was almost exhausted, and the state had been criticized for working inmates in mines. Two hundred prisoners moved from Brushy to Nashville. Brushy Mountain had held twice its capacity of inmates when the mine was worked because two men could use a cell for sleeping while another two worked a shift. When the mine closed the prison was automatically overcrowded. Warden Lake Russell reported that morale was higher after the mine closed, but the state had made no preparation for keeping the inmates busy. Officials made vague promises to build classsrooms and industrial workshops, but they took no action.

In 1969 the state reclassified all prisons. Brushy Mountain became a maximum security facility and Nashville a medium security one. The honor farm in Morgan County retained its previous status.

In 1972 guards at Brushy Mountain went on strike after two of them were disciplined. The two guards were union representatives; one was dismissed and one reprimanded. The strike was spontaneous rather than planned, but 150 guards walked off their posts, leaving a skeleton force to control the prisoners. State troopers manned the guard posts, and 400 inmates were immediately transferred to other facilities. Governor Winfield Dunn ordered the prison closed in July.

There were no serious negotiations between the guards' union and the state government. Prison Commissioner Mark Luttrell requested no funds at the end of the year to reopen the prison, and in early 1973 Governor Dunn announced the permanent closing of Brushy. He wanted to develop his regional prison idea as a substitute for the large state institutions. All former guards except the two union leaders were offered employment. Morgan County had supported Republican candidate Dunn in the 1970 election, giving him almost 300 votes more than John Hooker; but the guards believed that the closing of the prison had a political motive. They thought that the Democratic party would not have closed the prison.

Brushy Mountain employed 265 people when it closed, and this increased unemployment was a severe economic blow to Morgan County. The *News* lamented that the prison was the major employer of males in the county. Commissioner Luttrell and Representative Tommy Burnett met with the guards in 1973. Burnett, a Fentress County native who represented Morgan County in the General Assembly, and who was working to re-open the prison, had urged such a meeting. No results came from the negotiations, and state officials decided to sell the prison property. The two bids received were opened in January of 1974. One, for only $3000, was disregarded. Henry Melhorn and Willard Lane of Oliver Springs bid $61,006 for the prison, although they had no specific plans for its use. The state rejected this as too low and called for other bids, with a minimum bid of $100,000. None were received.

In 1974 Brushy Mountain Prison became a political football in the governor's race, as Governor Dunn had feared. Democratic candidate Ray Blanton promised to order a study and to open the prison if the study showed such action feasible. Republican candidate Lamar Alexander also said that he might re-open the prison. The county voted heavily for Blanton in the election—2388 votes for Blanton and 1348 for Alexander.

In March of 1974 newly inaugurated Governor Blanton ordered the prison opened; the first inmates arrived on May 15. These trusties cleaned and repaired the facility, readying it for occupation. A more extensive renovation of the prison in 1975 and 1976 cost the state about $2 million. The first ten guards reported for duty in August of 1975, and Clayton Davis, a native of Coalfield, was named deputy warden. Thus a major institution was again contributing to the county's economy.

After the prison opened, inmate unrest and escapes were frequent. Trusties walking away was a common occurrence, and serious disturbances broke the peace occasionally. In 1976 fourteen inmates, demanding a return to the Nashville prison, took a guard hostage for about eight hours before they were overcome by other guards. In 1977 the maximum security prisoners staged a strike; they were confined to their cells and denied working privileges. In June of 1977 James Earl Ray and six other prisoners attempted an escape over the back wall of the prison.

Ray was found about 54 hours later hiding under a bush in the mountains behind the compound.

Morgan County became home for a regional prison in 1980, built on the grounds of the old prison farm. There was some concern about the new facility interfering with the development of Frozen Head Park, but most Morgan County residents welcomed the new prison because of economic benefits. The impact of these benefits had been reinforced by the closing of Brushy Mountain between 1972 and 1975.

Conclusion

Morgan County's history is not unique. It has been a part of, and is a reflection of, the history of Tennessee and of the United States. Morgan County, to a large extent, is a microcosm of the nation.

One must admit after reading the story that Morgan County has had a difficult path to follow through its history, mainly occasioned by the natural hardships that the county's land and climate have imposed. The broken terrain, made more difficult by jagged peaks, was not even afforded the luxury of navigable rivers. The soil was relatively poor, and arable land was in short supply. The climate was not suited to some crops. Travel was arduous, settlement was sparse, and life was difficult.

Morgan County has experienced a very colorful history. The early settlements of Revolutionary War veterans, of Germans in Wartburg, of Englishmen in Rugby, and of Poles in Deer Lodge opened the county's history. The Civil War, with most of Morgan County supporting the Union, provided a costly interlude in the story. The building of Brushy Mountain Prison and the Cincinnati Southern Railroad added exciting pages to the saga. The struggle of Morgan County in the twentieth century to improve its economic position was inspiring.

Outsiders played a large part in the history of the county. They often provided the extra push needed to accomplish economic progress. The original settlers were outsiders, and, in their turns, the Americans, the Germans, the English, and the

The Obed River Gorge, typical of the scenic beauty of Morgan County. (Courtesy of Charles Kreis)

Poles all made their contributions. The Cincinati Southern Railroad provided an important outside catalyst for economic progress. The state of Tennessee, with its financial aid for highways and schools in the first part of the twentieth century, gave significant help. The federal government, with the New Deal and the Great Society, funded valuable projects and programs. Finally, outside manufacturing concerns coming into the county after World War II provided jobs.

One can logically conclude that the land in Morgan County and the outsiders coming in will provide the future of the county. The land, with its natural resources of timber, coal, and oil, can be exploited for additional wealth. The natural beauty of the land which drew the early settlers to it, however, will provide the newest and best source of wealth, drawing outsiders for vacations and for permanent residence. Morgan County can take its place alongside the Great Smoky Mountains as a leisure land for the large population in the eastern part of the United States. Frozen Head State Natural Area, Catoosa Wildlife Management Area, Big South Fork National Recreational Area, and Historic Rugby signal the beginning of new opportunities for the region. Outsiders will come in as tourists, developers, businessmen, and permanent residents to provide a new economic catalyst for Morgan County.

Suggested Readings

Belissary, C. G. "Tennessee and Immigration," *Tennessee Historical Quarterly*, 7 (Sept. 1948), pp. 229–248.

Biggs, R. D. "Cincinnati Southern Railroad," *East Tennessee Historical Society*, no. 7 (1935), pp. 81–102.

Boniol, John D. "The Old Walton Road," *Tennessee Historical Quarterly*, 30 (Winter 1971), pp. 402–412.

Campbell, Mary E. R. *The Attitude of Tennesseeans Toward the Union, 1847–1861*. New York: Vantage, 1961.

Cooper, Hobart S. "German Swiss Colonization in Morgan County," unpublished M.A. thesis, University of Tennessee, 1925.

Eller, Ronald D. *Miners, Millhands, and Mountaineers*. Knoxville: University of Tennessee Press, 1982.

Glenn, Leonides D. *The Northern Tennessee Coal Field*. Nashville, 1925.

Goodspeed, W. A., ed. *History of Tennessee*, East Tennessee Edition. Nashville: Goodspeed Publishing Co., 1887.

Hughes, Emmy. *Dissipations At Uffington House: Letters of Emmy Hughes*. Memphis: Memphis State University Press, 1976.

Hughes, Thomas. *Rugby*. New York: MacMillan, 1881.

Hutson, A. C. "Overthrow of Convict Lease System in Tennessee," *East Tennessee Historical Society*, No. 8 (1936), pp. 82–103.

Justice, C. C. "Morgan County's Unique History, " *Knoxville Sentinel*, April 28, 1925.

Killebrew, Joseph B. *Introduction to the Resources of Tennessee*. Nashville: Taves, Eastman and Howell, 1874.

Knox, John B. *The People of Tennessee*. Knoxville: University of Tennessee Press, 1949.

Lacy, Eric R. *Vanquished Volunteers: East Tennessee Sectionalism*. Johnson City: East Tennessee State University, 1965.

McElwee, W. E. "The Old Road," *American History Magazine*, 8 (1903), pp. 347–354.

Morris, Eastin. *The Tennessee Gazeteer*. Nashville: W. H. Hunt, 1834.

Muir, John. *A Thousand Mile Walk to the Gulf*. Boston: Houghton Mifflin, 1981.

Phelps, Jewell. "Cumberland Plateau,"in Fullerton, R. O. *et al*, *Tennessee*

Geographical Patterns and Regions. Dubuque, Iowa: Kendall Hunt, 1977.

Seymour, Digby Gordon. *Divided Loyalties: Fort Sanders and the Civil War in East Tennessee.* Knoxville: University of Tennessee Press, 1963.

Stagg, Brian. *The Distant Eden: Tennessee's Rugby County.* NP: Paylor Publishers, 1973.

———, *Deer Lodge, Tennessee: Its Little-Known History.* Oak Ridge, 1964

Tennessee State Planning Commission. *A Study of State Institutions: Brushy Mountain Penitentiary.* Nashville, 1937.

Tennessee Valley Authority. *Emory River Valley: Summary of Resources,* 1968.

Whiteaker, L. W. "Civil War," in *Encyclopedia of East Tennessee.* Oak Ridge, 1981.

Winton, Ruth Nellie. "A History of Brushy Mountain Penitentiary." unpublished M.A. thesis, University of Tennessee, 1937.

Works Projects Administration. *Tennessee: A Guide to the State.* New York: The Viking Press, 1939.

Wright, J. C., ed. *Autobiography of Reverend A. B. Wright.* Nashville: Cramston and Curtis, 1896.

Wust, Klaus. *Wartburg: Dream and Reality of the New Germany in Tennessee.* 31st Report, Society for History of Germans in Maryland. Baltimore: J. H. Furst, 1963. (Copy in Tennessee State Library & Archives, Nashville.)

Index

Illustrations are indicated by an asterisk following the page number.

About the Author

Born in northeast Texas in 1938, Calvin Dickinson earned his bachelor's and master's degrees in history at Baylor University. Living in eastern North Carolina for ten years, he taught at Chowan College and earned his Ph.D. in history at Chapel Hill. In 1971 he accepted a position at Tennessee Technological University in Cookeville, where he teaches history and studies the Upper Cumberland region of the state. Particularly enjoying the scenic outdoors and the vernacular architecture of the area, he is fascinated by the history of the people.

He coedited and coauthored *The Heritage of the Upper Cumberland,* the first book to deal with the history of this region. He has been director or consultant for numerous projects studying the history and heritage of the area. He has also codirected a study of the Watauga region of northeast Tennessee and has published a number of articles about that area of the state.

In his other academic interest, England, he has published one book, *James Harrington* and a number of essays concerning the history of eighteenth century England.